ISBN 978-1-7325402-3-1

Published by Hardy Perennial Press LLC
1645 W. Valencia Rd #109-154 Tucson Az 85746

Catalina Mountains:
A Guide Book with Original Watercolors
by
Frank S. Rose

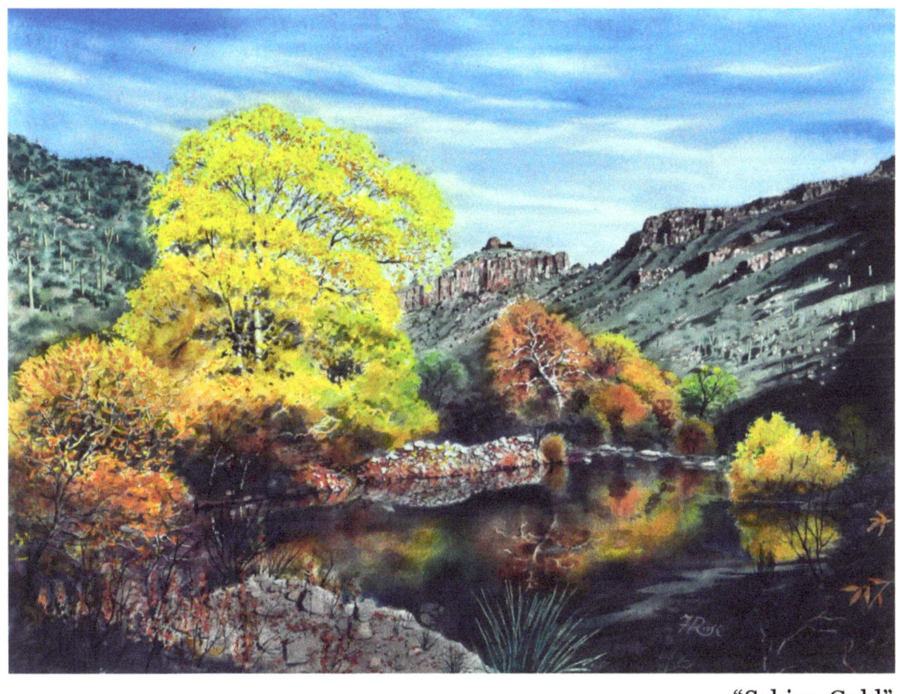

"Sabino Gold"

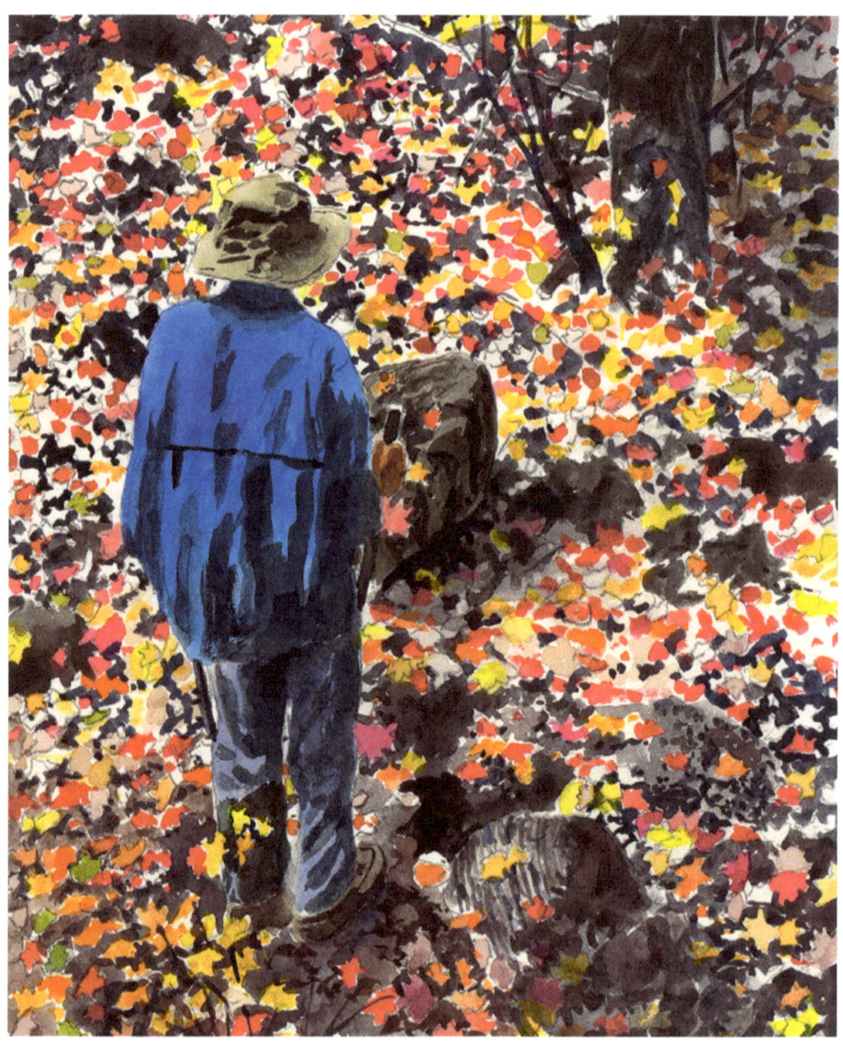

In October Ed and I especially enjoy walking in Marshall Gulch where the forest floor is carpeted with fallen leaves. In this painting the leaves are all from Big Tooth maples. There are two other areas we like to visit to see the fall colors: Turkey Run with a connection to the Aspen Trail, and Bear Wallow. Aspens and Big Tooth maples provide the most spectacular show in all three of these sites. Lower down the mountain willow trees, sycamores and velvet ash provide their own show.

CONTENTS

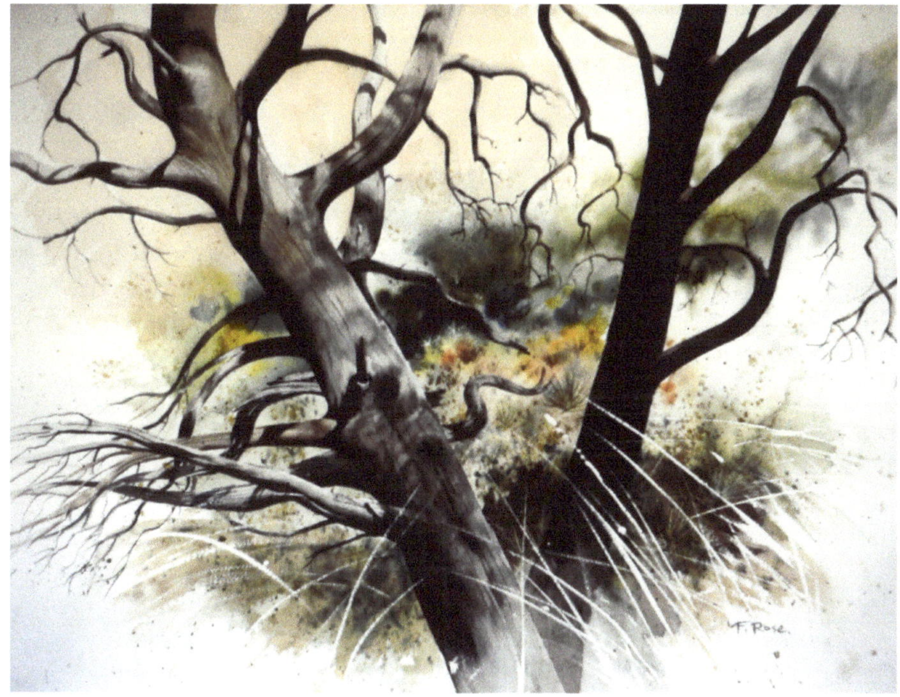

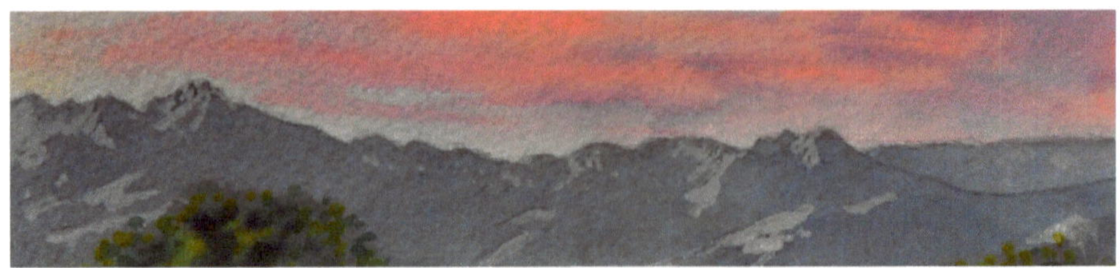

PREFACE

When I want peace, contentment and healing, I go to the mountains. Fortunately the base of the nearest range is just under seven miles from our home. I have taken this trip more than a thousand times since my wife and I moved here in 1982. In that time I have done hundreds of paintings. The landscape pictures form the main part of this book, many of them now in private collections. I also include portraits of flowers that might be seen in that part of the range.

On my first visit to Tucson, in April of 1982, my friend, Kathlyn, took me up the Mount Lemmon highway, and treated me to a ride on the ski lift. I knew at once that these mountains would be a significant part of my life here. My wife and I moved to Tucson that same summer, and before long had discovered the joy of hiking in Arizona. At that time I was the pastor of a church on Country Club Road. We eventually sold our little church and moved to Wrightstown Road. One of the great attractions of the lot was its view of the mountains. In designing the church we asked the architect to provide a thirty-two foot wide panoramic view of the mountains(seen above and at the top of the following page). The worship space became very special for our Sunday congregation and for the hundreds of weddings, memorial services and other events held there. So much of that was due to the magnificent view of the mountains.

For many summers Louise and I have rented various cabins in Summerhaven for a week or more. The weather pattern involved clear mornings, with clouds building up during the late morning for afternoon showers. Accordingly we planned to hike in the mornings. In the afternoons I painted and Louise wrote. One of the great challenges of the artist is to decide what subject matter to use for his or her art.

One year, I think it was 1999, I decided to paint the many wildflowers on the mountain. I had no idea of their names, but I could photograph them and use the photographs as a basis for a series of flower portraits. After a while I met Joan Tedford who not only had made a plant list for the mountains (as she has done for other places), but also invited me on the summer plant walks led by Bob Porter. Eventually I switched back to photographs as being a lot quicker and more detailed

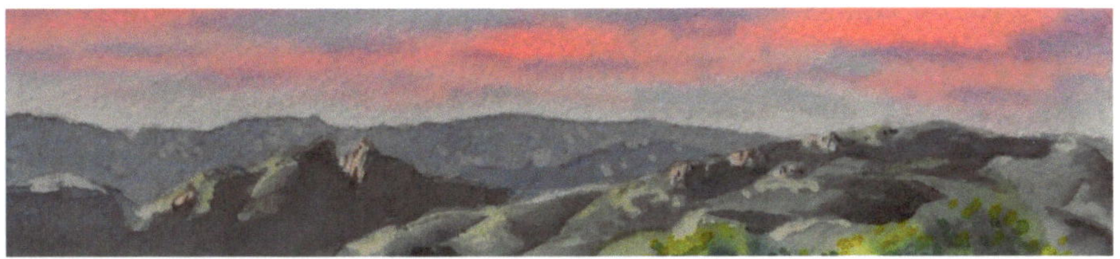

than my paintings, and published a book of the wild flowers, mostly of the Catalina Mountains. This was followed by a book on Mountain Trees.

In 2004 I teamed up with Edward Gelardin. Ever since then we have regularly hiked the mountains, with a special interest in identifying and enjoying the wild flowers. In addition to flower paintings, I have done many watercolors of scenes in the mountain range. He suggested that these paintings might well be made into a book, which became this guide to the mountains.

Arizona is ranked third in the 50 United States for its biological diversity. And the Santa Catalina Mountains have the most plant species of any of the Sky Islands.

There are two reasons why I paint from photographs.

1. Some of the views are taken from a vantage point that has foot or vehicle traffic, so that I cannot sit in the same spot for the hours required to do justice to the scene.

2. In nature the light changes so fast that only a photograph can capture a particular scene. The picture enables me to take my time painting in the studio.

ROAD COURTESY

A double yellow line runs along the Hitchcock Highway, broken only briefly, in three places. They made pull offs along the highway to allow people to pass. I regularly look in my rear view mirror to see if there are any vehicles behind me that would prefer to go faster than me. I then look for the next pull off which is usually less than a mile away. This is a courtesy for them, and makes my drive up the mountain more pleasant.

On holidays there might be a continuous line of traffic, which means that the simplest thing is then to just stay in line and enjoy the scenery.

When the road was widened in 1988 to 2005, a bicycle lane was added. Some days there are hundreds of cicylists enjoying this special place. I love seeing them, and am happy to share the road with them. The speed limit on the mountain is 35 miles per hour. Many cyclists exceed that on the way down the mountain.

From the base of the mountain it is a fifty-mile round trip to Summerhaven. There are no gas stations on this road, so it is good to plan accordingly.

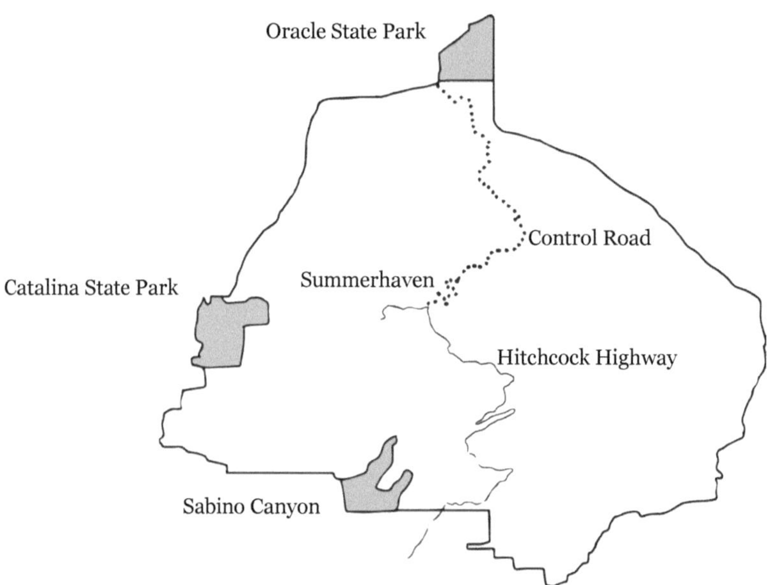

The Santa Catalina Mountain Range

It would be impossible to do justice in pictures to a range covering 200 square miles, with an elevation difference of well over a mile (about six and a half thousand feet). This is not merely because of its vastness, but also because of the changing light conditions throughout a day or year.

The Greek philospoher Heraclitus once said "No man ever steps in the same river twice, for it's not the same river and he's not the same man." By the same reasoning, you cannot visit the same mountain range twice. You also cannot *see* the same mountain twice, especially since the light on it is constantly changing and the mountains themselves are evolving over time.

How old are the Santa Catalina Mountains? This question does not allow for a simple answer. Some of the rocks in the mountains are 1.65 billion years old (Pinal Schist). It seems to have been part of the Laramide orogeny (began 70 to 80 million years ago, and ended 35 to 55 million years ago). The main upheaval that forms the core of the mountain range goes back about 35 million years. There was further development 26 million years ago, and again 15 million years ago. Unlike many of the other sky islands, this range is a dome. The top is a flat meadow, not a peak, (unlike the Santa Rita mountains to the south). If you include Agua Caliente Hill and the Rincon Mountains, it forms the largest of the sky islands of Southern Arizona, with the most biological diversity. It is also the most accessible, with a road leading to the very top. This road offers some of the most spectacular views in Arizona.

In the pages that follow I also include a small watercolor portrait of a flower that may be seen on that part of the mountain along with its common name and scientific name.

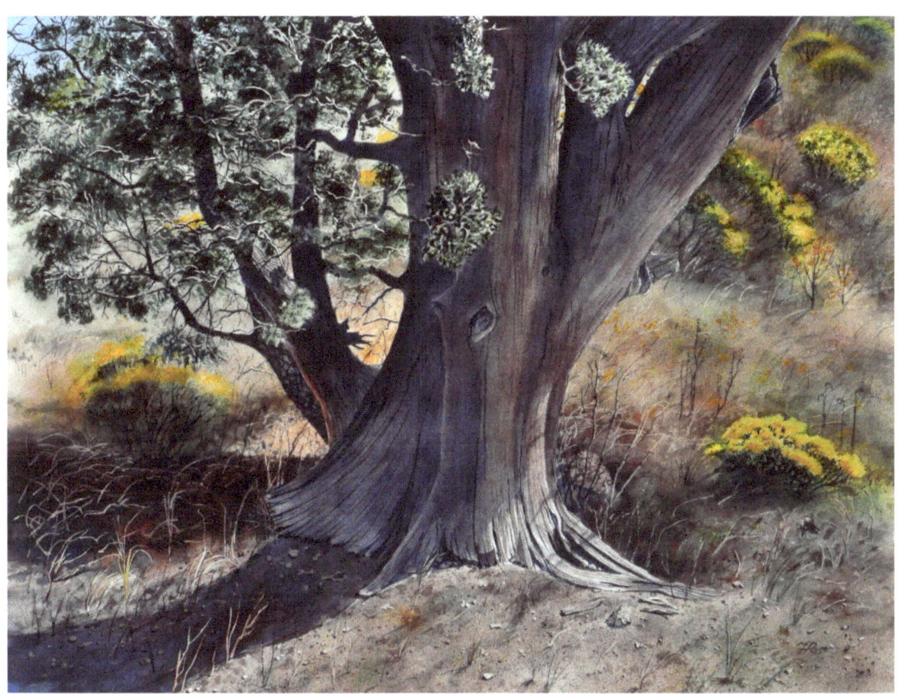

MOUNT LEMMON

In 1881 John Gill (1831 or 1832-1908) and Sara (Plummer) Lemmon (1836-1923) were on their honeymoon. They took the train to Tucson, and tried three different times to scale the mountain from the South. Then they contacted Emerson Oliver Stratton (1846 -1925) a miner in Oracle, who took them up the mountain on horseback. They were both botanists and Sara was also a watercolor artist. He was a Civil War veteran, having spent the last months of the war in the infamous Andersonville prison. Emerson named the highest peak Mt. Lemmon in her honor, as the first non-native to reach the top. He carved this fact on one of the ponderosa pines.

NOTABLE DATES

Unknown date - Range named Babat Do'ag
1697 - Range named Sierra de las Santa Catarina
1848 - End of Mexican-American war
1850 - New Mexico became a territory
1854 - Arizona and parts of the SouthWest acquired in the Gadsden Purchase
1863 - Arizona (once part of New Mexico) became its own Territory
1870's to 1880's - Rest area during Apache wars
1880 - Start of mining in the range
1881 - The highest peak named Mt. Lemmon
1902 - National Forest established
1908 - First cabin built in the mountain range
1912 - Arizona became the 48th State of the Union.
1918 - Control Road finished
1928 - Lemmon Rock Lookout built
1933 to 1950 - General Hitchcock Highway built
1939 - Founding of Summerhaven
1950 - Tricot Road build to carry electricity to the top
1978 - Congress set aside 56,933 acres of wilderness
1988-2005 - General Hitchcok Highway rebuilt
2003 - Aspen fire

Chapter One:
Viewing the mountains from below

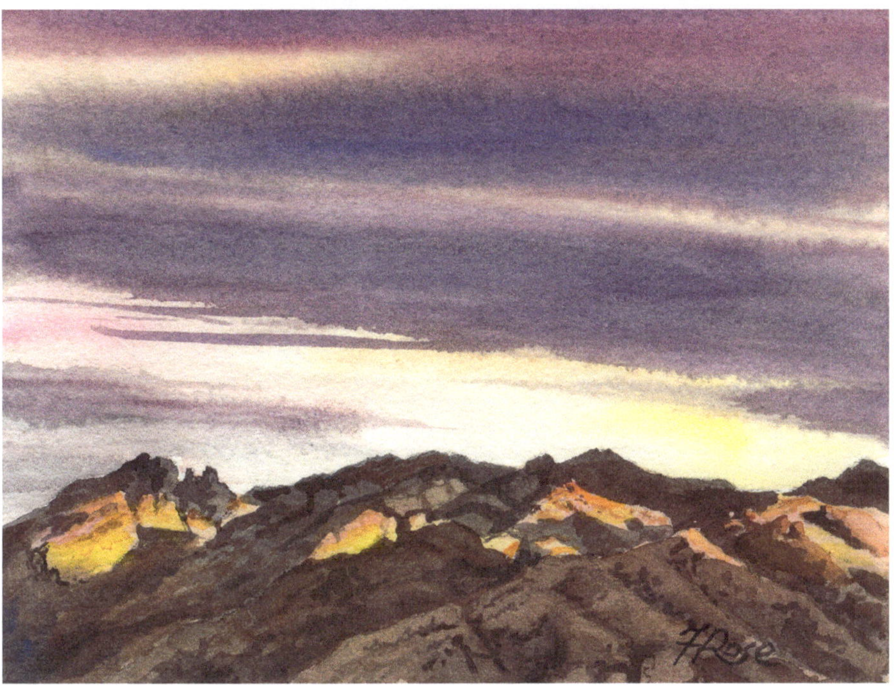

The main portion of the city of Tucson lies in a valley surrounded by mountain ranges. To the West are the Tucson mountains, with the beautiful Gates Pass. On the other side of the pass you find the movie set of Old Tucson, and the Arizona Sonora Desert Museum.
To the South are the Santa Ritas, with Mt. Wrightson, the highest peak visible from Tucson at 9456 feet, and Mt. Hopkins with its observatory. To the East are the Rincon Mountains, which are attached to the Santa Catalinas, with Agua Caliente Hill lying between. Then to the North are the Santa Catalinas themselves.

There are about a million people living with a view of this mountain range, which looks very different depending on where you are and what the weather is like as well as the time of day. The morning sunrise on the mountains makes dramatic patterns of light and dark. Prominent Point and Finger Rock are on the left in the painting above. In the middle are Window Rock and Cathedral Rock, and just coming into view on the right is Rattlesnake Peak.

Prickly Poppy
Argemone pleiacantha

1

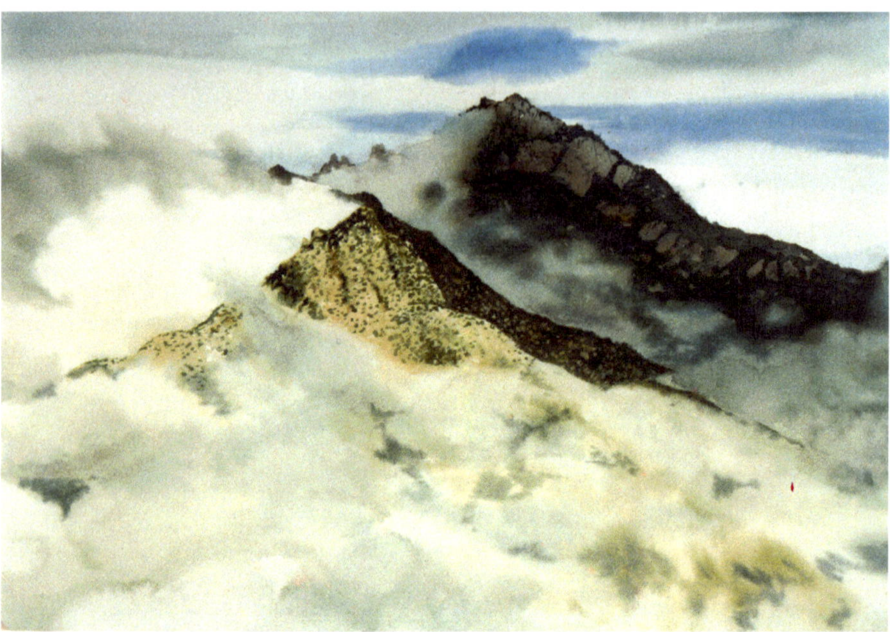

Cathedral Rock, at 7952 feet, is the tallest mountain in the front range of the Catalina Mountains. It is also the most rugged. Clouds add mystery to this view.

Back in 1984 I went into an establishment and before getting to the point of my visit, mentioned to the receptionist that the mountains looked particularly beautiful that day. She replied: "They're nothing but a pile of dirt and rocks." I wasn't quick enough with a reply, but since then I have often thought that this pile is one of the most interesting places in Arizona, full of life and beauty.

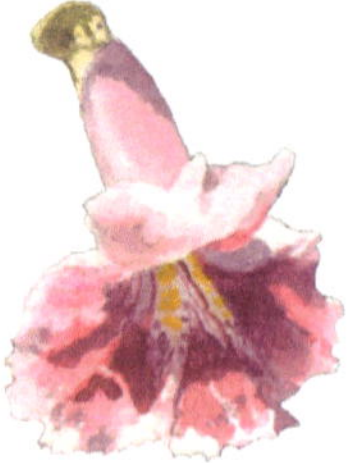

Desert Willow
Chilopsis linearis

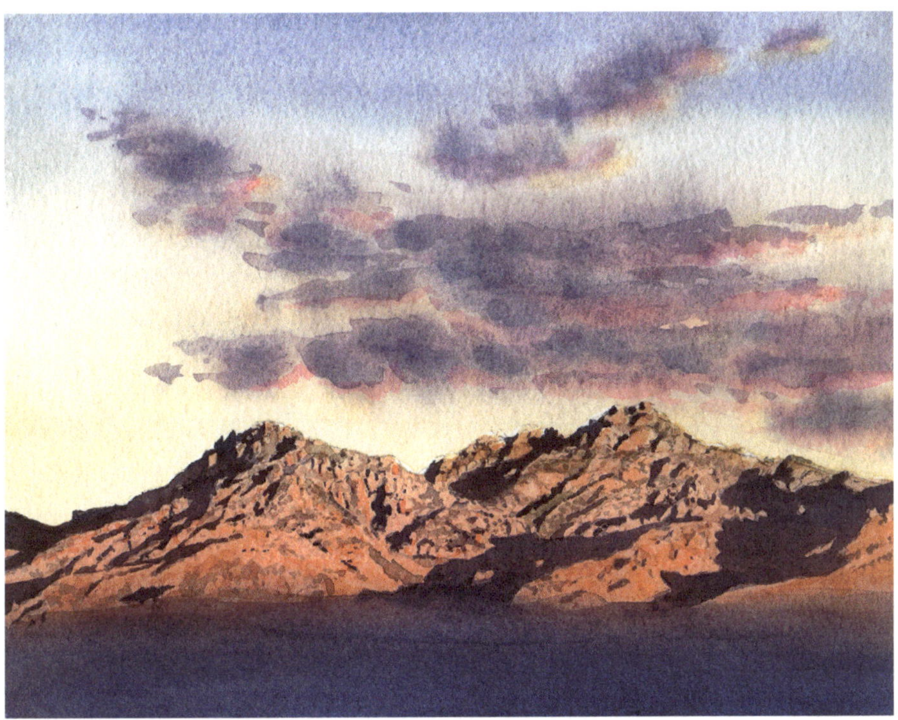

The highest peak in this painting is Cathedral Rock. The peak to the
left is Window Rock, named for a natural arch about 25 feet wide and
15 feet high. It is visible from a number of places in the Western part
of Tucson. The spanish word for Window is Ventana, which explains
the name of the luxury resort at its base.

In 1985 my wife and I hiked from Sabino Canyon up to a point between Cathedral Rock and Window Rock so that I could perform a
wedding in the Window. It was quite an adventure, especially since
it took place in the middle of June and
the temperatures in the valley rose to 109
degrees.

The mountains catch the morning sun
while most of the city is still in shadow as in
this painting.

Twist Flower
Streptanthus carinatus

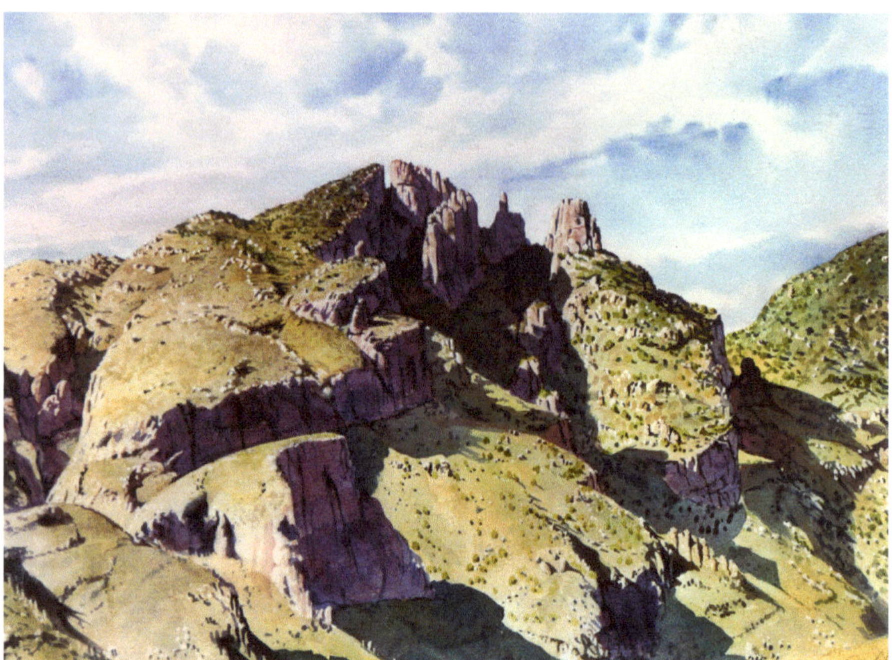

The dome here is called Prominent Point. To its right is Finger Rock, a one hundred foot spire. Strangely enough, the Finger Rock/Mount Kimball trail does not go to the Finger. It rises on the other side of the valley from this formation, and goes to the top of Mt. Kimball (hidden from view on the right side of this picture.)

Mt Kimball is covered with trees, so the one time I managed to hike that high (7255 feet) I could not get a view from the top, but there was plenty to see on the way up and back.

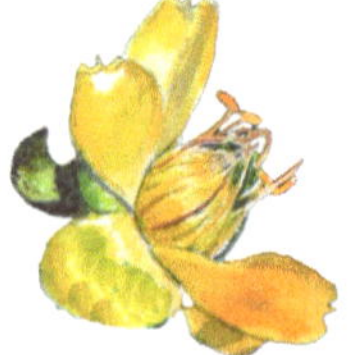

Creosote Bush
Larrea tridentata

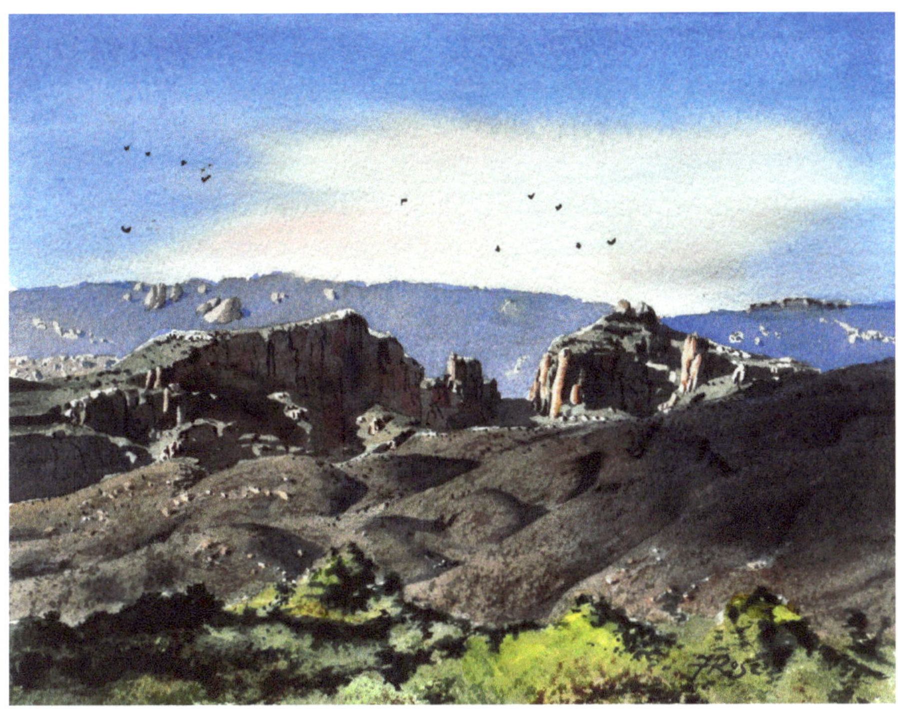

This is a view of the mountain as you travel North on Houghton Road.
On the left you can see Blackett's Ridge. One of my friends hikes it
every week. The few times I have climbed it were quite strenuous.
The trail begins in Sabino Canyon and goes 2.3 miles to the peak
(4409 feet). At the top you can look across to Thimble Peak, one of the
landmarks on the front range. The birds are taking their early evening
flight.

The highest point in the range, Mt. Lemmon, is seen below the group
of birds on the left side of this painting. The top is flat. In 1954, the Air
Defence Command built a Radar Station there.
It is now part of the University of Arizona, and is known as *Mt. Lemmon Sky Center Observatory* with seven telescopes. It is open for
tours that need to be reserved ahead of time.

Cleveland Sage
Salvia clevelandii

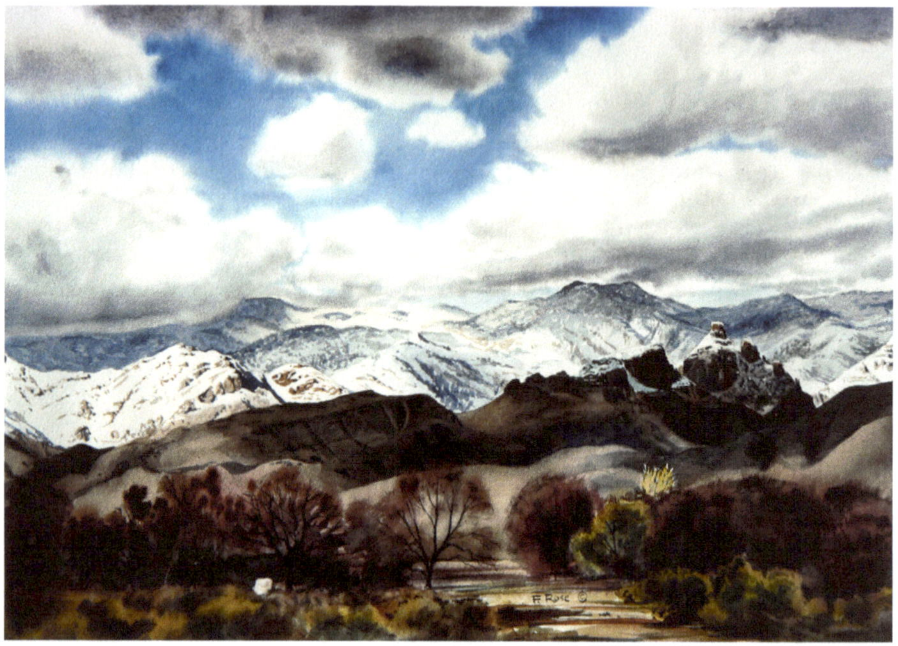

The mountains take on a special charm after a winter snowfall. There can be several feet of snow at the top of the mountain. Those looking from the south side of the range notice how quickly it disappears from view. Then a drive up the mountain reveals lots of snow on north-facing slopes and in shaded areas. I have seen patches of snow near the top of the mountain as late as May when Tucson temperatures can reach a hundred degrees.

There is enough rain and cold weather to have snow in Tucson. But since rain is infrequent, and so is the cold weather, it is relatively rare to have both conditions, so snow is seldom seen in the valley. When it falls it does not stay on the ground very long. Every year there is snow high in the mountains, sometimes six feet deep or more. Our birdbath in the valley has ice on it several times each winter.

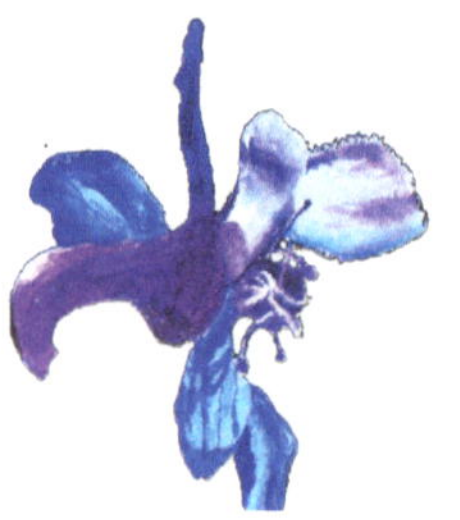

Desert Larkspur
Delphinium scaposum

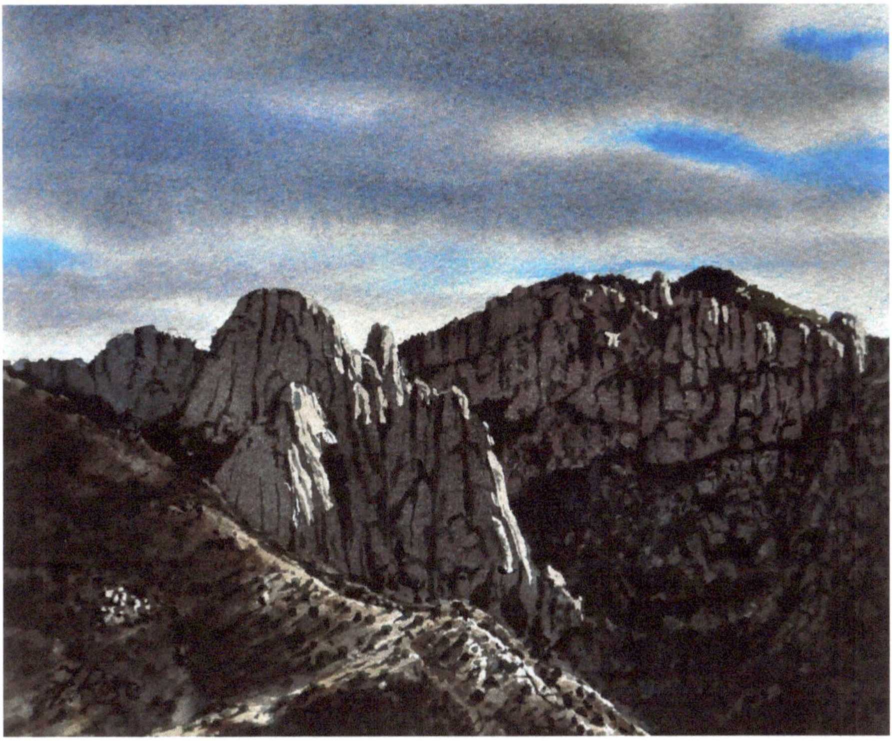

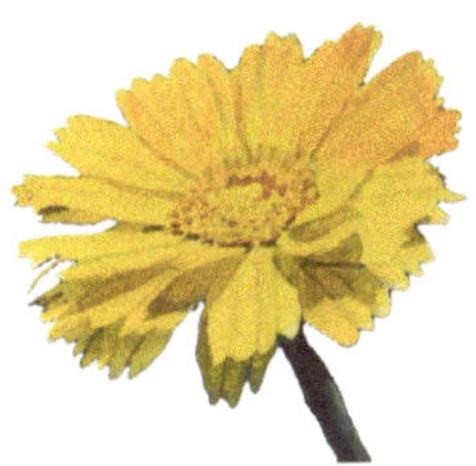

There are many wonderful rock formations on the North side of the mountains. These are visible from Oro Valley and Catalina State Park. The skyline on this North face of the range is more dramatic than the one seen from the central parts of the city of Tucson.

The Westernmost portion of the range is Pusch Ridge, to the right in this view. It is now home to a flock of Big-horn sheep that was reintroduced to the range in 2013. More were introduced later, and the sheep have reproduced. The flock has grown to over 100 individuals in 2018.

Desert Marigold
Baileya multiradiata

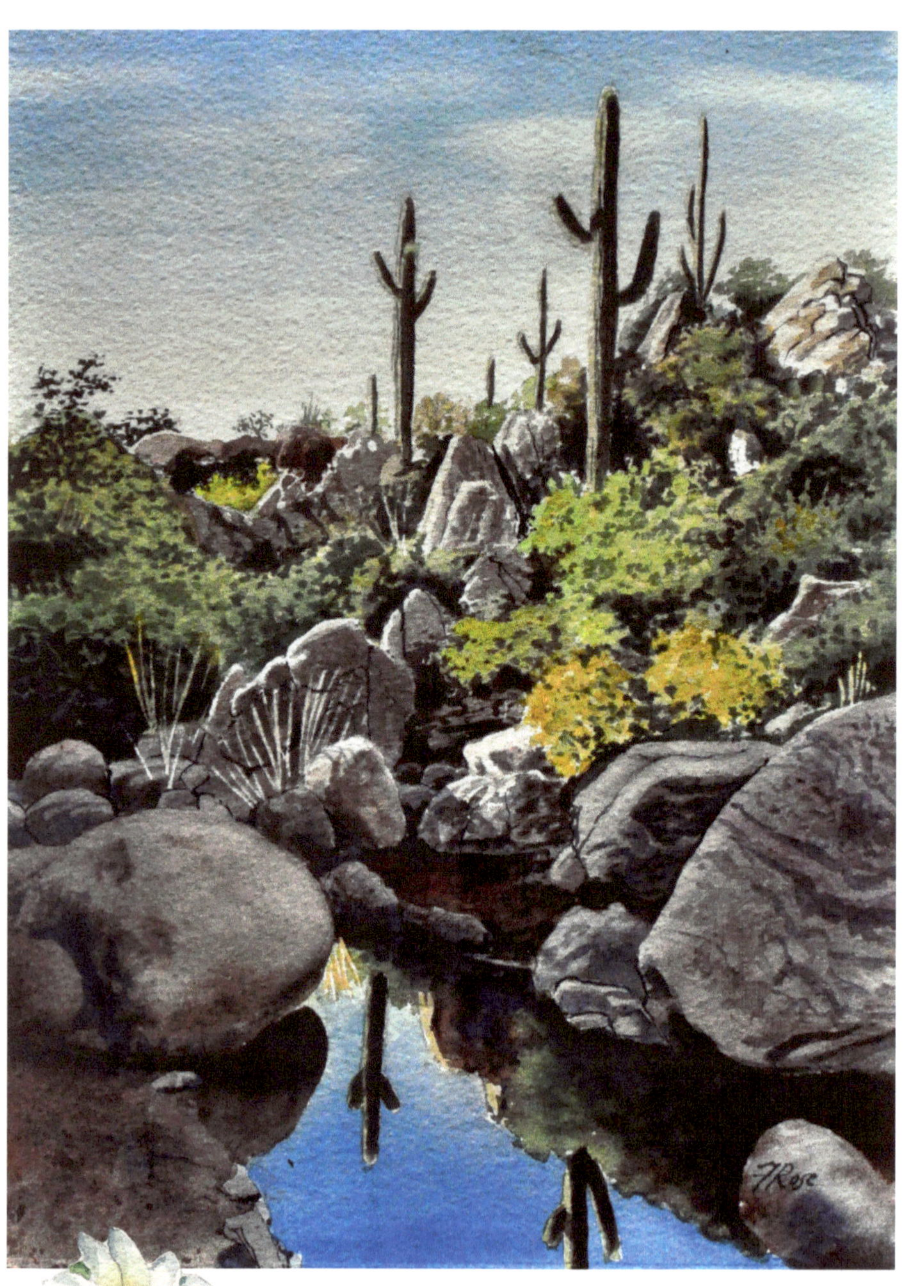

Saguaro
Carnegiea gigantea

There are a number of access points to the mountain range from below. **Sabino Canyon** on the South side of the range and **Catalina State Park** on the West side are the areas with the greatest number of visitors.

SABINO CANYON

The most popular of all the areas accessible directly from the valley is Sabino Canyon. Sabino Creek, that feeds the canyon, begins very high in the mountains. It flows much, but not all, of the year, sometimes so furiously that it is difficult to cross.

Sabino Canyon is a favorite for hikers, cyclists, and casual visitors. It has a gift shop, nature trails, picnic areas, and many trail heads. There are two tram rides, one going directly up the canyon, which runs about every half hour, and the other that goes over to Bear Canyon that runs hourly.

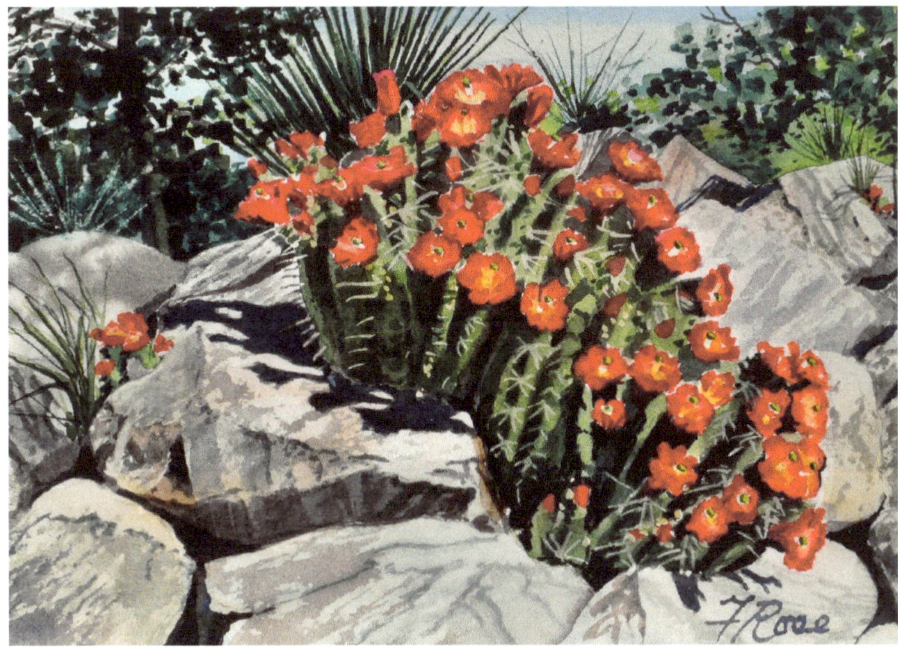

Claret Cup Cactus
Echinocereus triglochidiatus

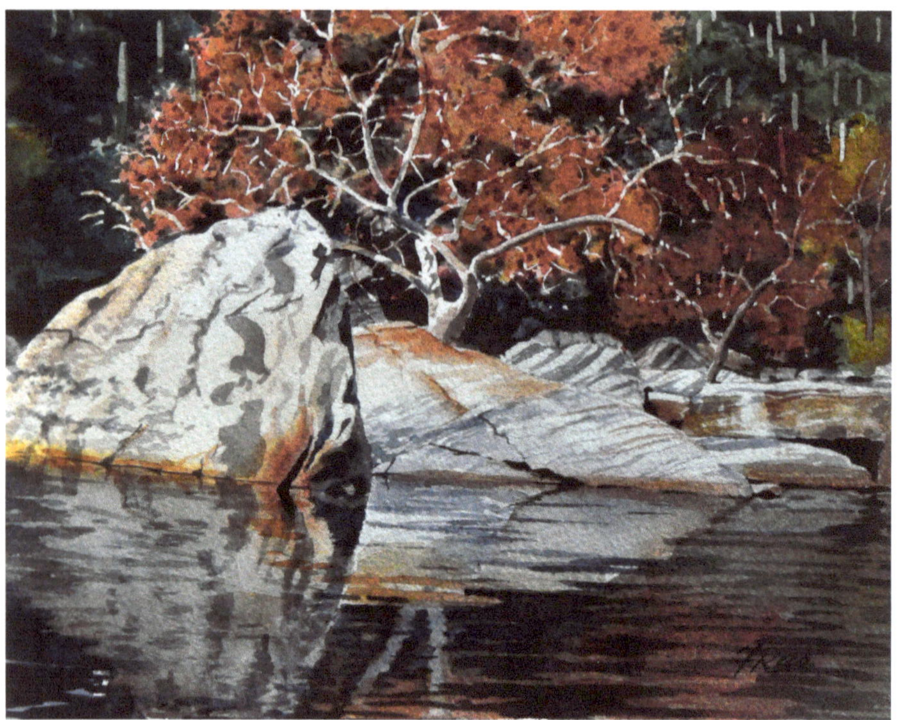

The road up Sabino Canyon was built by the CCC during the depression, and includes 9 bridges that cross and recross Sabino Creek in about a four-mile stretch. The distinctive rocks with different colored stripes tumbled down during the great earthquake May 3, 1887, a 7.6 magnitutde earthquake in Mexico (about 40 miles south of Douglas). This was the only earthquake in recent history to do any significant damage in Arizona.

Years ago I was riding the tram back down the gorge when my eye caught this view as we crossed the bridge between stops four and three. I was struck by the light on the rocks and the Sycamore standing out against the dark background. I returned the next evening to take some pictures from which I did this painting. Since then the sycamore has died. Now there are a number of Cottonwood trees in this area.

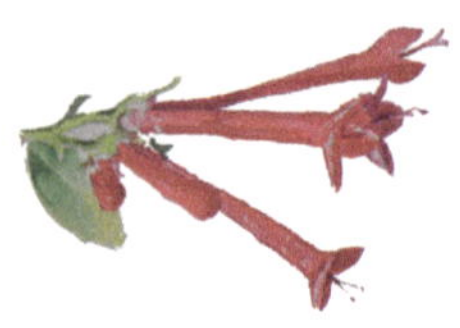

Smooth Bouvardia
Bouvardia ternifolia

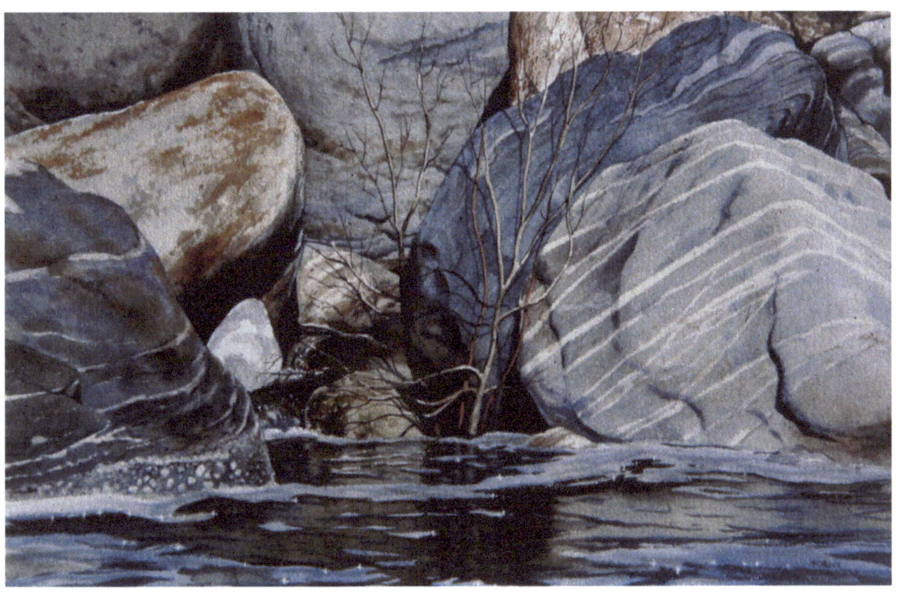

Water levels in Sabino Canyon vary enormously from season to season. The flow is particularly strong when the mountain snows melt in the Spring, and during the Monsoon rain season in late Summer.

Years after taking watercolor lessons from Jack Reid, of Ontario, Canada (when we lived there), he and his wife, Maggie, came to Tucson for a visit. He especially loved Sabino Canyon with the wonderful forms of rock and water. We went out painting together several times, and never tired of this delightful area.

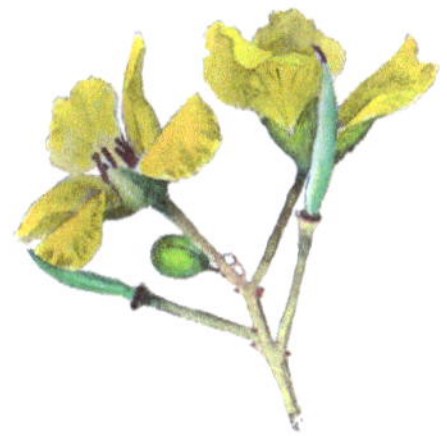

Desert Senna
Senna covesii

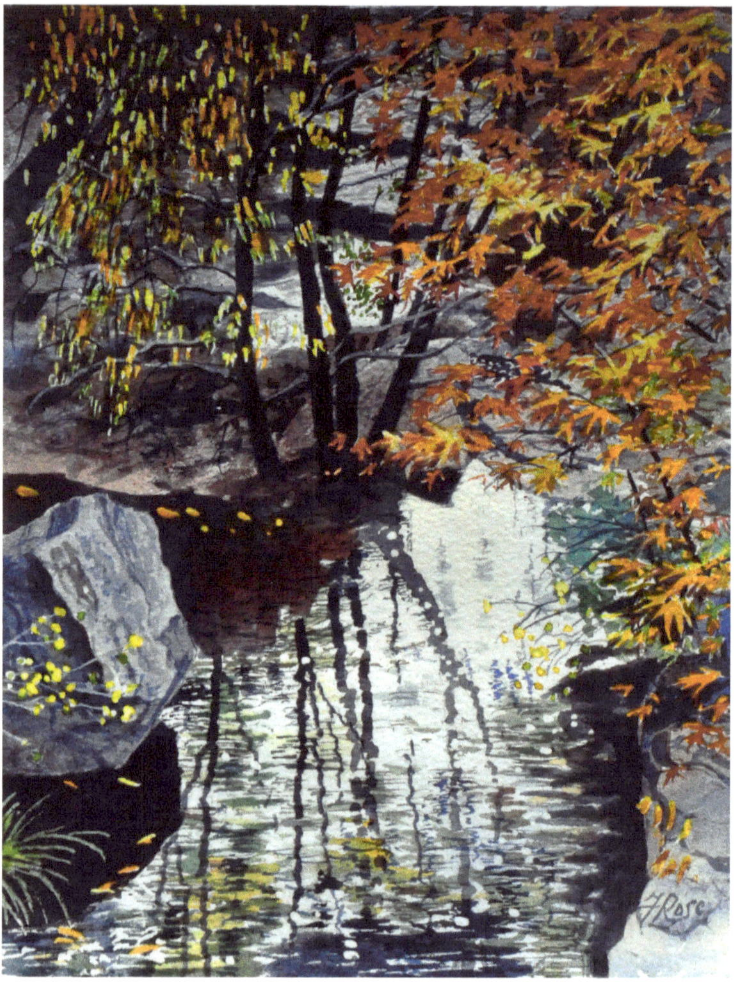

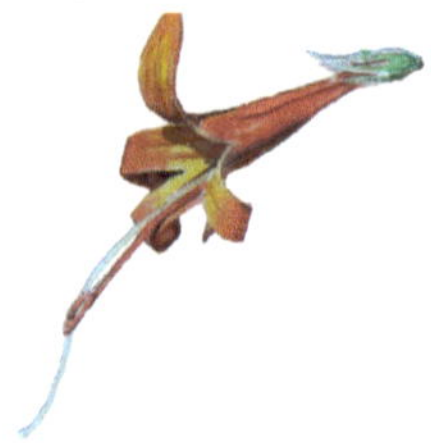

Taking the tram one October, I found a number of intriguing scenes to paint.

This is a view looking downstream as the tram crossed one of the nine bridges. It was late in the afternoon, with the warm sunlight accentuating the rich fall colors.

There are many weeks when the bridges are covered in water, but not too deep for the tram to cross. In those times people will ride the tram to go through the water and then walk along the road between the bridges.

Desert Honeysuckle
Anisicanthus thurberi

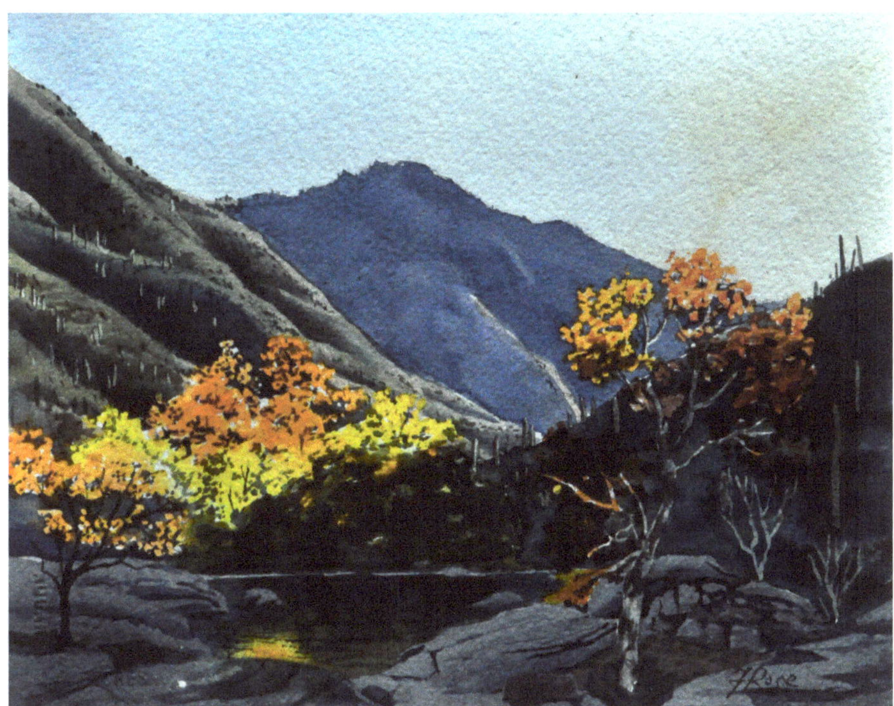

Early morning cyclists and pedestrians are allowed to go up and down the road. There is a visitor's center and gift shop near the parking lot. This is also a center for the Sabino Canyon Volunteer Naturalists, who lead nature walks for people of all ages.

Sabino Canyon is beautiful any time of the year. My favorite is the Fall, which extends well into the Winter months. There is usually water left over from the Summer rains, and lots of color provided by the Cottonwoods, Velvet Ash, Willow and Sycamore trees.

This is a view looking South from about the middle of the canyon. In October and November the evenings are cool, and sun shining in the West brings a glow to the fall colors. Thousands of people enjoy running and walking the road and trails, and, at certain hours, even cycling. It is a prime beauty spot.

Button Bush
Cephalanthus occidentalis

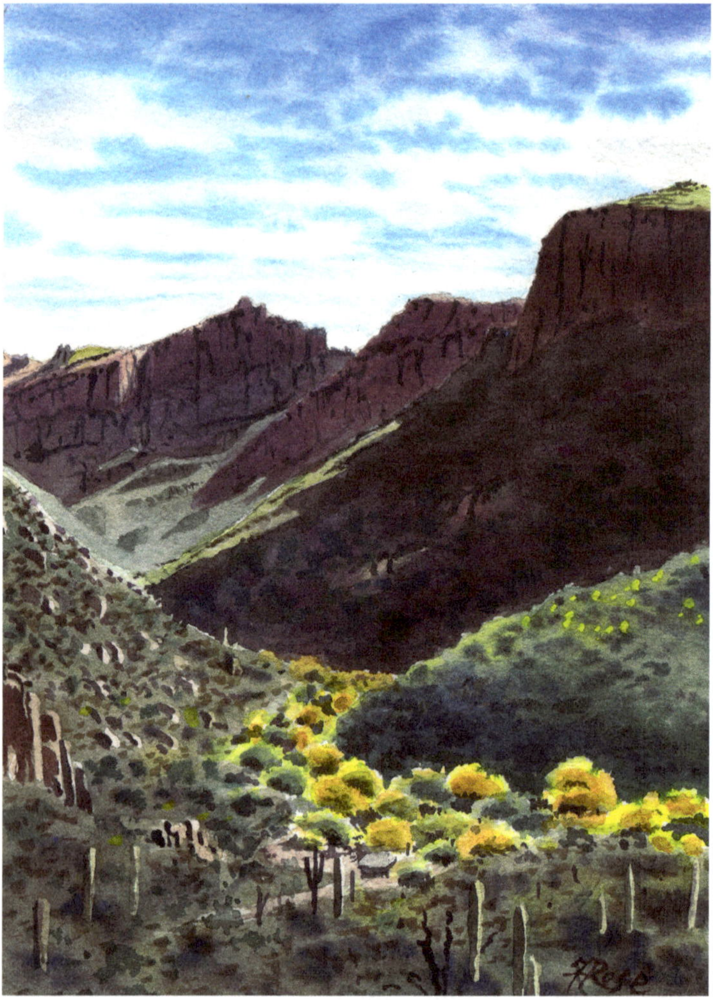

This is the view at the end of the Bear Canyon tram ride. The road continues down the slope to a lean-to by the cottonwood trees where the trail starts. Thimble Peak is in clear view most of the way to the Falls. The top of the Thimble is 5,322', just a little over a mile above sea level.

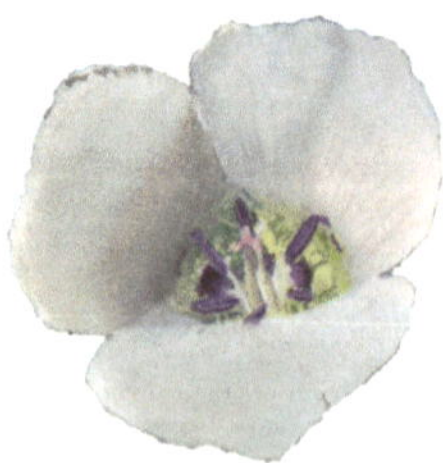

Doubting Mariposa Lily
Calochortus ambiguus

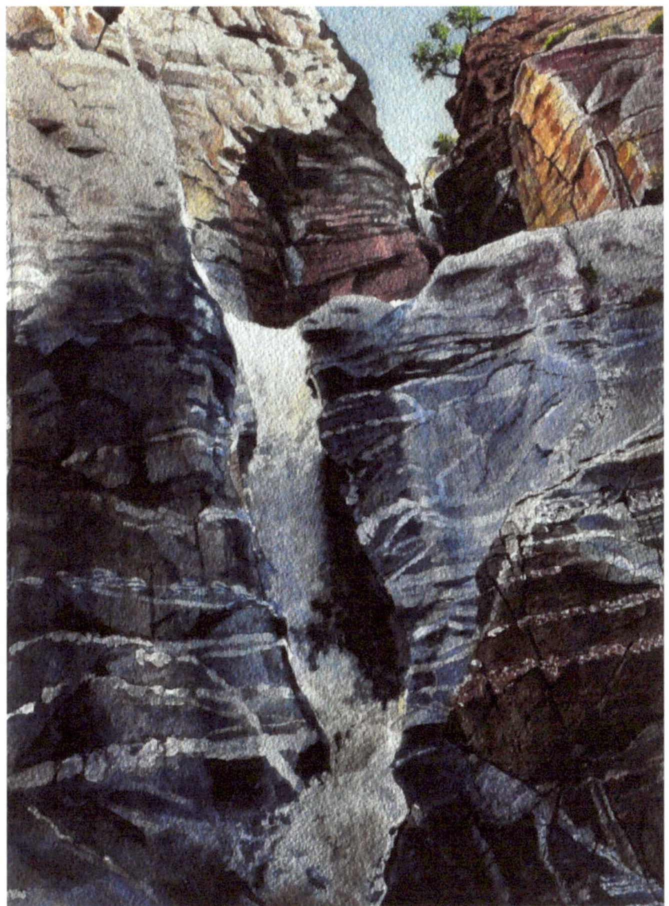

SEVEN FALLS

Two tram routes leave from the visitor's center. The main one goes up Sabino Canyon with 9 stops and many crossings. Sometimes the bridges are overflowing.

There is another less frequent tram that goes to Bear Canyon, where you can get off at the turn-around point and walk the additional 2.5 miles to Seven Falls, a beautiful and very popular area.

When the falls are flowing at their greatest, it is challenging to reach them since the trail crosses the stream many times.

Ocotillo
Fouquieria splendens

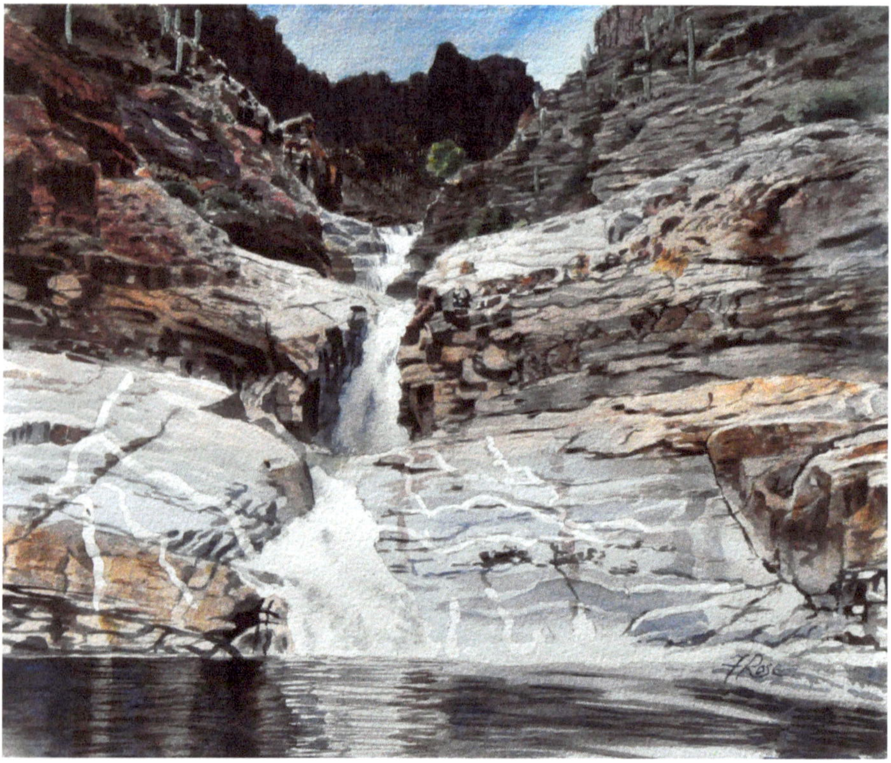

Seven Falls provides quite a challenge for an artist. I decided to do two paintings from the pictures I took on this trip. The painting on the previous page is a close-up of the central portion of the falls seen from a slightly different angle.

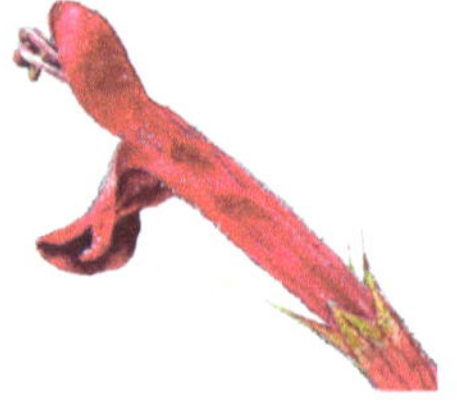

Texas Betony
Stachys coccinea

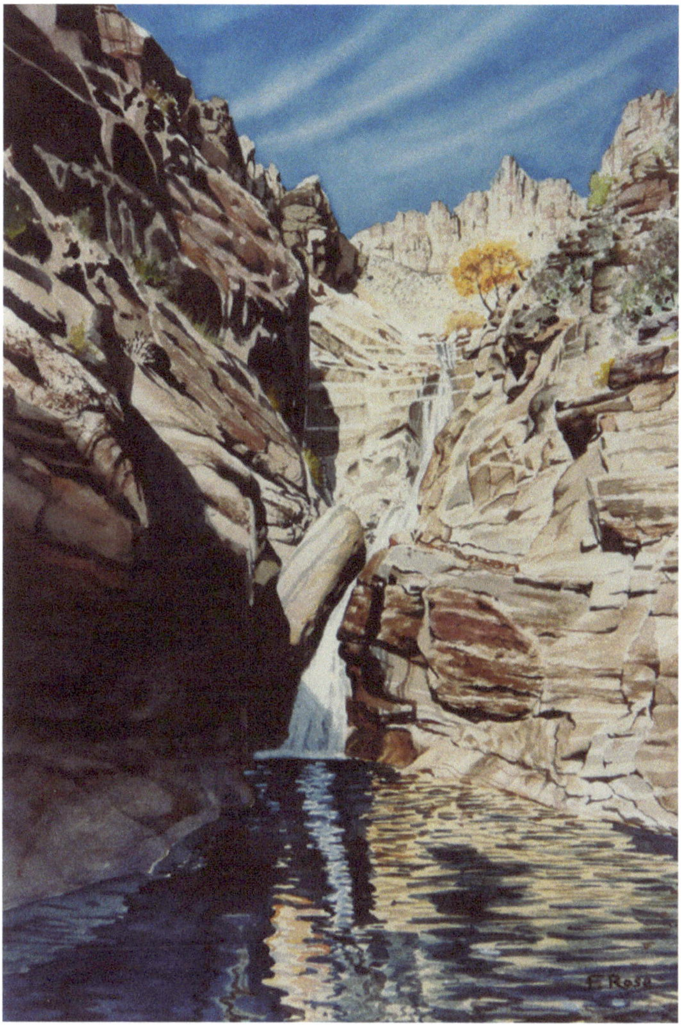

This painting shows a portion of the falls. The striations in the rock are typical of the Catalina banded Gneiss (pronounced "nice") which is the main rock formation in the front range of the mountains.

The vertical format helped me to convey something of the height of the cascade and the way the water enters the beautiful pool at the bottom. After possibly getting overheated on the trail, people enjoy a cool dip in this mountain stream.

In the Spring and Fall there is a steady flow of hikers exploring this very special area.

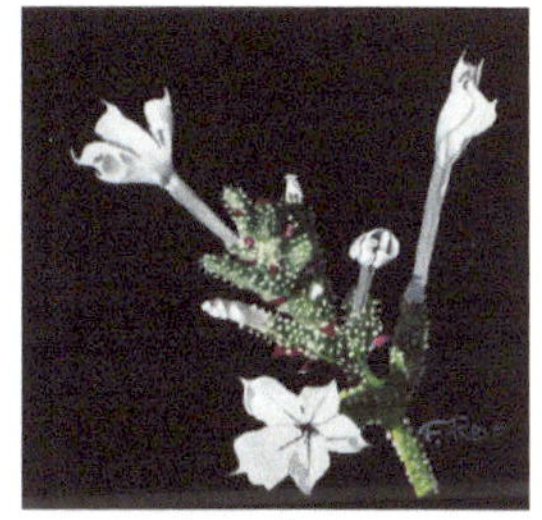

Leadwort
Plumbago zeylanica

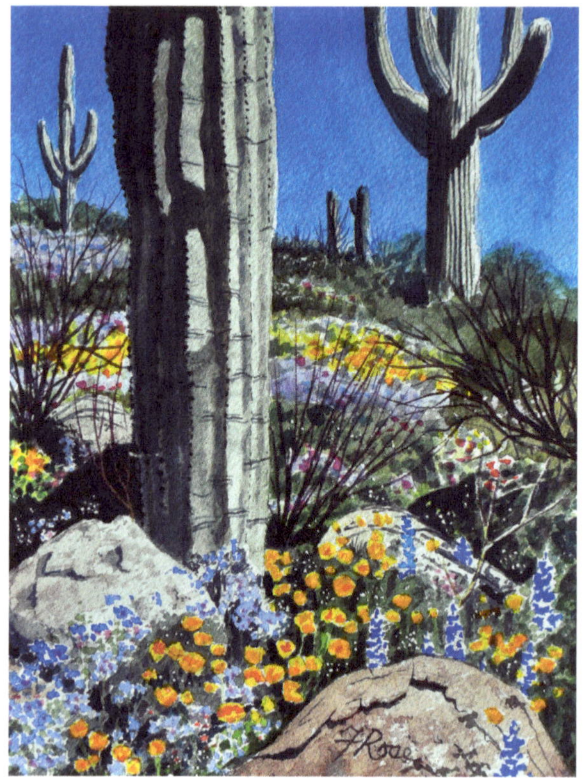

CATALINA STATE PARK

Long before coming to Arizona I had heard of the show of flowers called the desert in bloom. Catalina State Park is one of the best places to see this. Winter rains make for a good showing of Spring blooms, the best ones occurring after having some rain every month from November to March. That does not happen every year. When it does there are crowds of people walking the trails.

Spring flowers include the Mexican poppy, three different species of Lupine, Owls' clover, Chicory, Desert Marigold, Phacelia, Brittlebush and so on and on. There are close to four hundred flowering species in this beautiful park.

There are a number of horse trails as well as hiking trails in the park. Some of the trails can take you from here to the very top of Mt. Lemmon. The park opened in 1983

Desert Mariposa Lily
Calochortus kennedyi

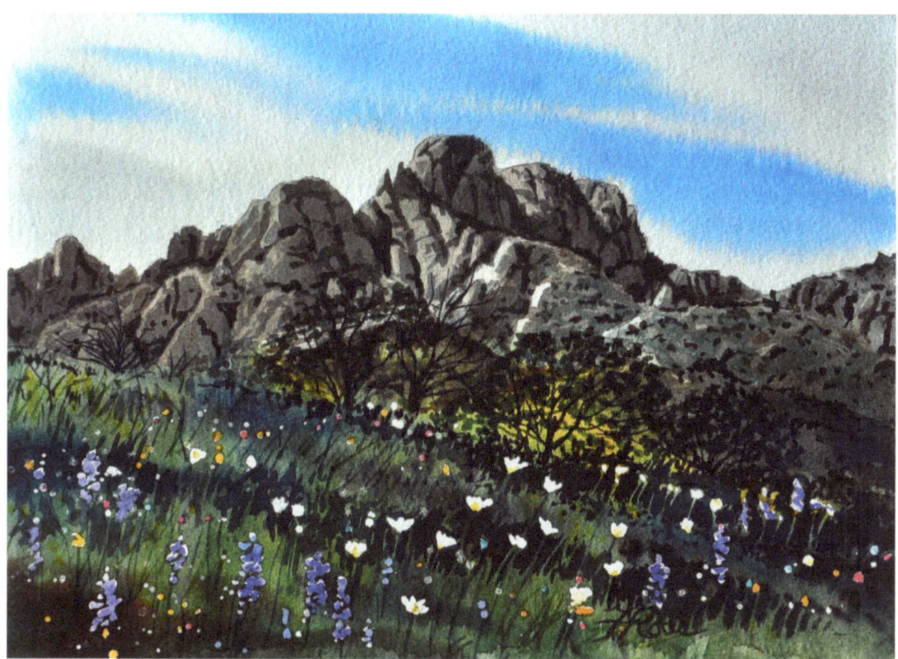

The mountain range is more dramatic viewed from Catalina State Park than from the south. Here are some of the other flowers that make up the Desert in Bloom, the blue Lupines, white California Chicory, Blue Dicks and Pine-leaf Milkweed (in the cameo below). In peak years the show is quite breath-taking with masses of gold and accents of red, blue and white flowers.

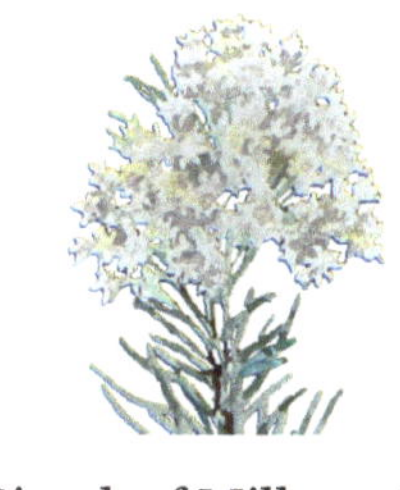

Pine-leaf Milkweed
Asclepias linaria

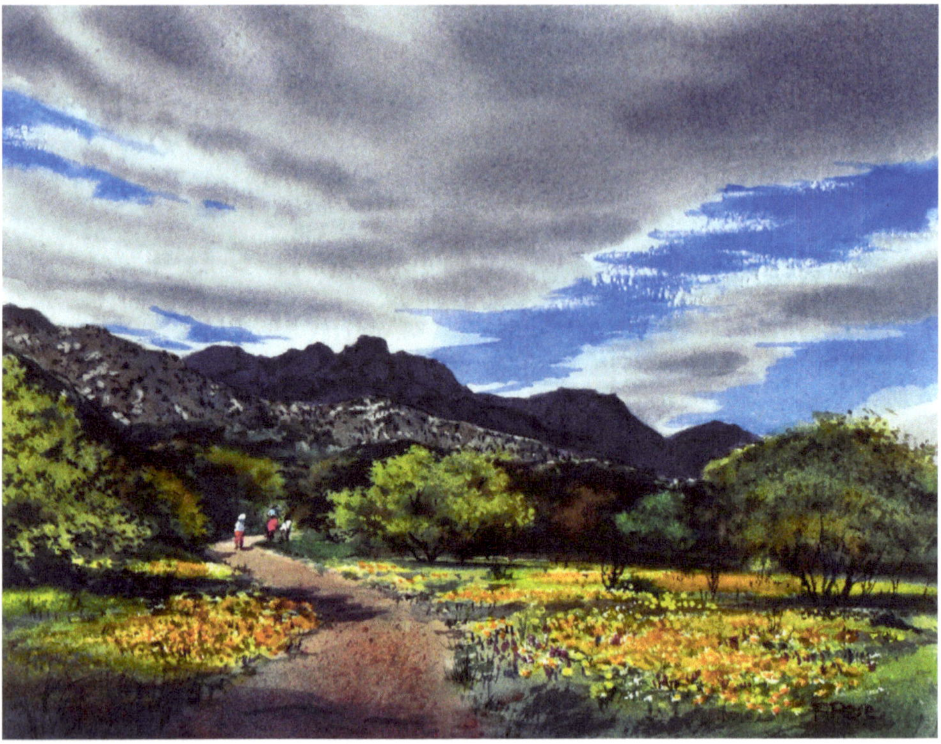

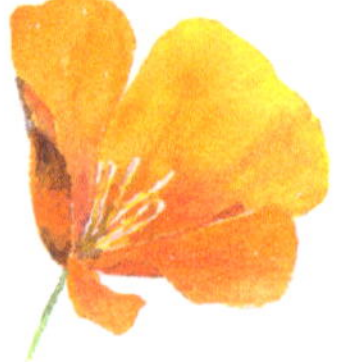

2017 was a wonderful year to see the desert in bloom. The figures in the distance are to represent our grown children who happened to be visiting Arizona at that time of maximum Spring beauty.

This is a view looking West as we returned to the parking lot. The peak on the right of this picture is Pusch Ridge. The flowers are mostly Mexican Gold Poppies.

Mexican Gold Poppy
Eschscholzia californica

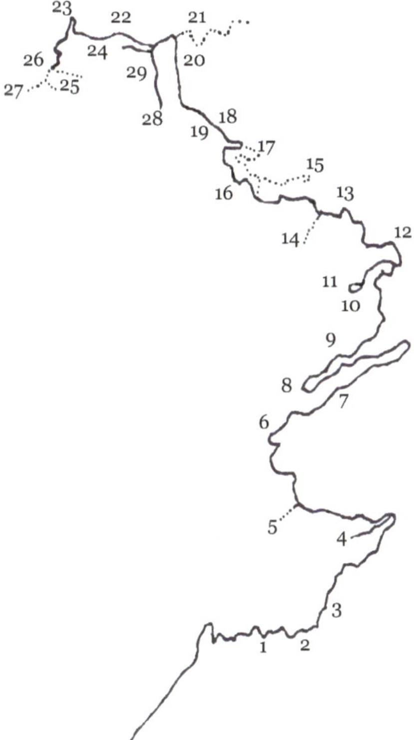

Chapter Three:
A guided tour up Catalina Highway

This is one of the most interesting and beautiful roads in Arizona, providing easy access to a variety of life zones, and offering wonderful views. It is also criss-crossed with a number of hiking trails, preeminently the Arizona Trail, that begins at the Mexican border, and ends at the border with Utah for a total of about 800 miles. There are two main routes of the Arizona Trail on this mountain range, each with its own special charm.

When I first looked up at the Catalina Mountains from the valley, the grey-blue areas looked like some kind of moss. I knew that I was looking at a forest, but it was very difficult to convince myself that these patches were trees, some of them more than a hundred feet tall.

Driving up the mountain highway, the temperature drops about one degree per mile. This provides for a changing environment that supports a variety of living things. There are different plants at the top of the mountain than there are at the middle or bottom, and different animals, birds and insects.

Coral Bean
Erythrina flabelliformis

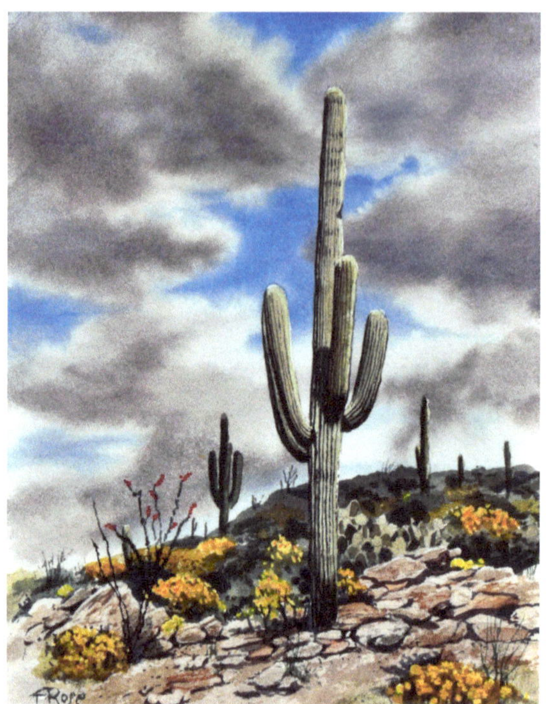

1. BABAT DO'AG

The first pull-off on the right is called Babat Do'ag from, the Tohono O'Odham name for the range. It means "Frog Mountain" possibly referring to the fact that the range, seen in profile, is flat like a crouching frog.

This is a favorite place to watch the sunset. The Baabat Do'ag trail begins across the road and goes a few miles up the mountain. The first part of the trail is steep and rocky. It is also a wonderful area for seeing Spring flowers, like the Brittlebush in the painting. As I walk this trail, I suspect that part of it was once a road. At the end of the trail you can look down and see Molino Canyon Vista and part of Molino Basin far below you.

In 1697 Father Eusebio Kino (1645-1711) named the mountain range the Sierra de las Santa Catarina (after St. Catherine). Later this was anglicized to the Santa Catalina Mountains. It is often referred to as Mt. Lemmon, but that is simply the highest peak. There are many other mountains in the range, notably: Buster, Evans, Gibbon, Green, Guthrie, Kellogg, and Mounts Bigelow and Kimball plus Table Mountain. There are also many named Peaks, Rocks, and Knobs.

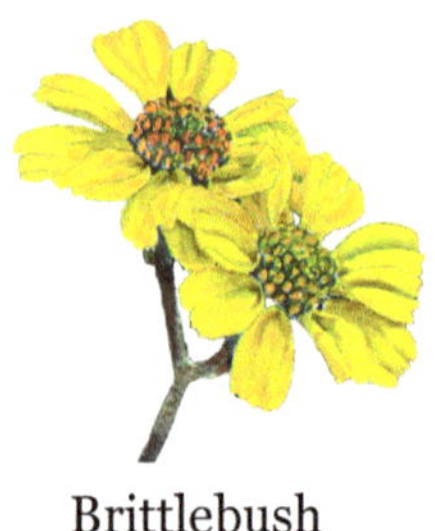

Brittlebush
Encelia farinosa

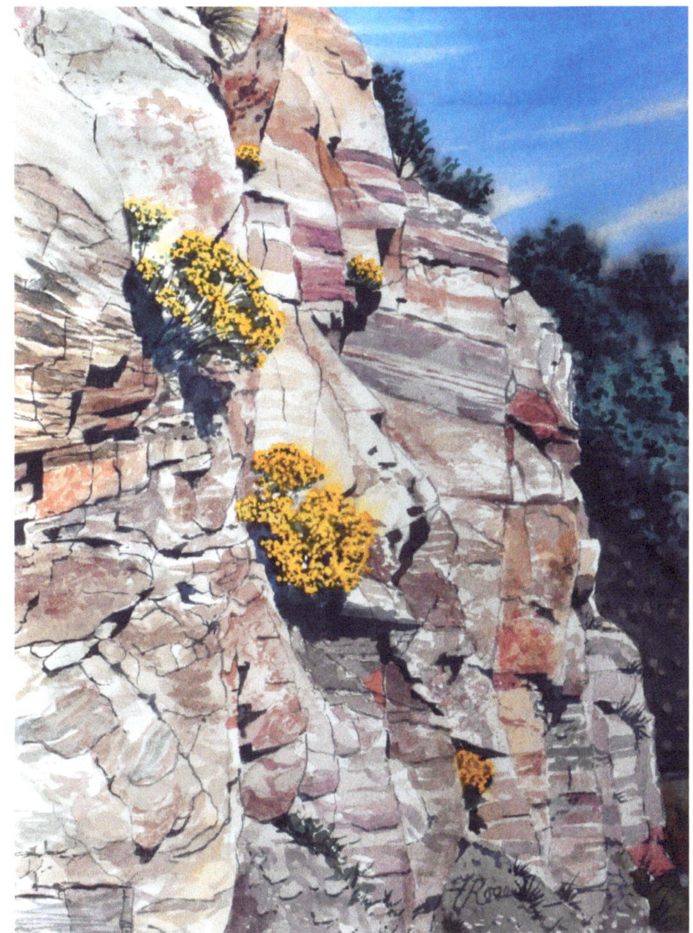

2. MILE POST FOUR

The Turpentine bushes are in flower late in the summer. The name indicates that the leaves have the smell of turpentine. After the Summer flowers have faded, this evergreen shrub comes into bloom. It is found in the lower parts of the mountain, mostly from about mile post 3 to 8. It grows on the ground or hanging on to cliff faces, as in this picture. The variegated color of the stone shows that it is Catalina Banded Gneiss. When you reach this part of the road you have left behind views of the valley, and are now in the range itself.

An Arizona Rosewood tree seems to be hanging on for dear life to the rocks in the middle right of the picture. There are a few Saguaro cactus along this part of the road but they are thinning out.

Turpentine Bush
Ericameria laricifolia

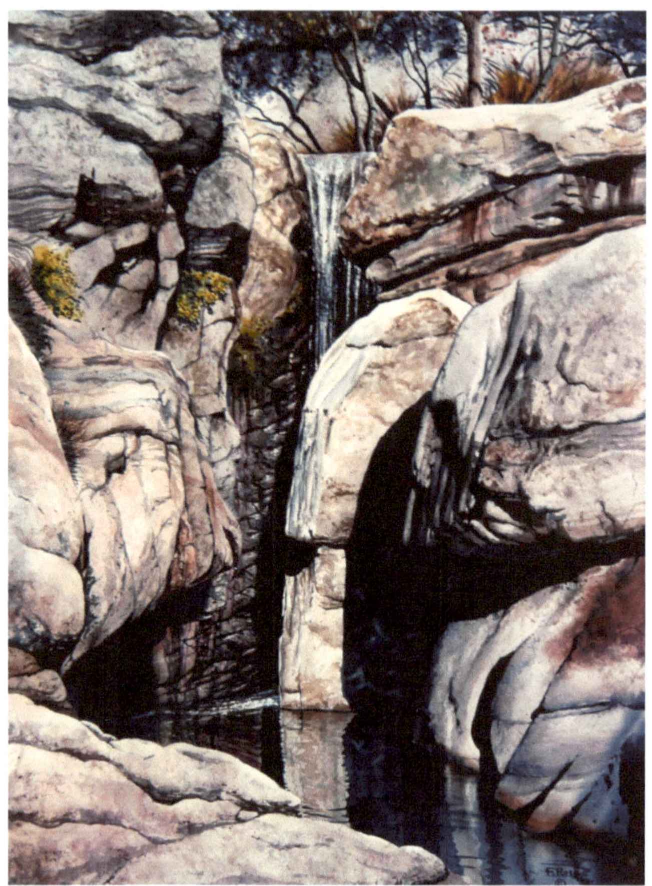

3. MOLINO CANYON VISTA

The second pull-off on the right going up the mountain is Molino Canyon Vista. This takes you to a beautiful area where the Molino Creek has a waterfall that's around sixteen feet tall. I have not seen a name for it. I call it "Hidden Falls" because of the way the view of the cascade is blocked by boulders.

The first time I painted the falls I got to a point where I needed more photographs. I returned a few weeks later only to find that the falls were completely dried up and were not running again for several months.

There is a paved walk here with nature signs. The stream bed is a great place to see riparian trees, like the Arizona Sycamore, Velvet Ash, Fremont Cottonwood, Walnut and Hackberry. There is also an abundance of wildflowers.

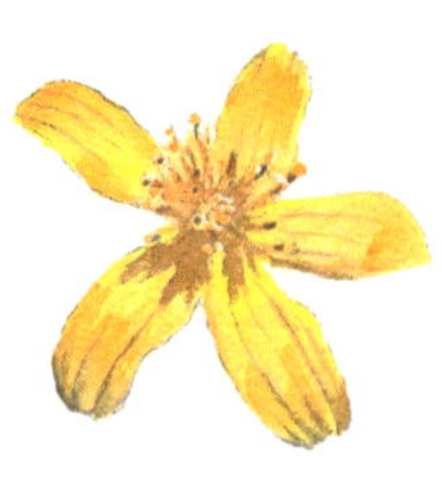

Apache Beggarticks
Bidens aurea

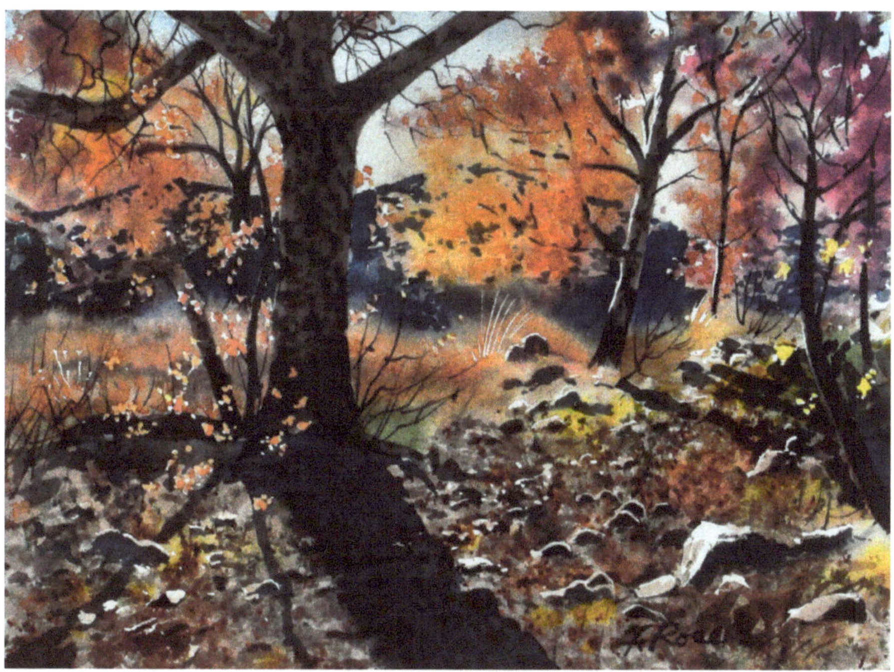

The stream that feeds "Hidden Falls" does not run year round. Sometimes there are puddles here and there, but little surface flow. In long periods of drought it seems that there is no water for the trees, but it flows underground, otherwise trees like the Arizona Sycamore above, and other riparian trees, could not survive here.

One of the most spectacular flowering plants is the Sacred Datura whose large, white flowers open in the evening and close late the next morning, each one surviving only one day. The plant is toxic.

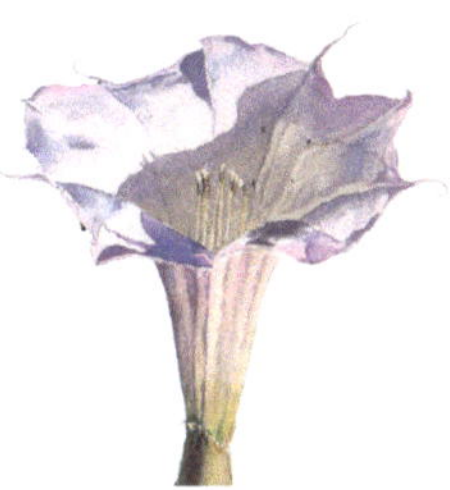

Sacred Datura
Datura wrightii

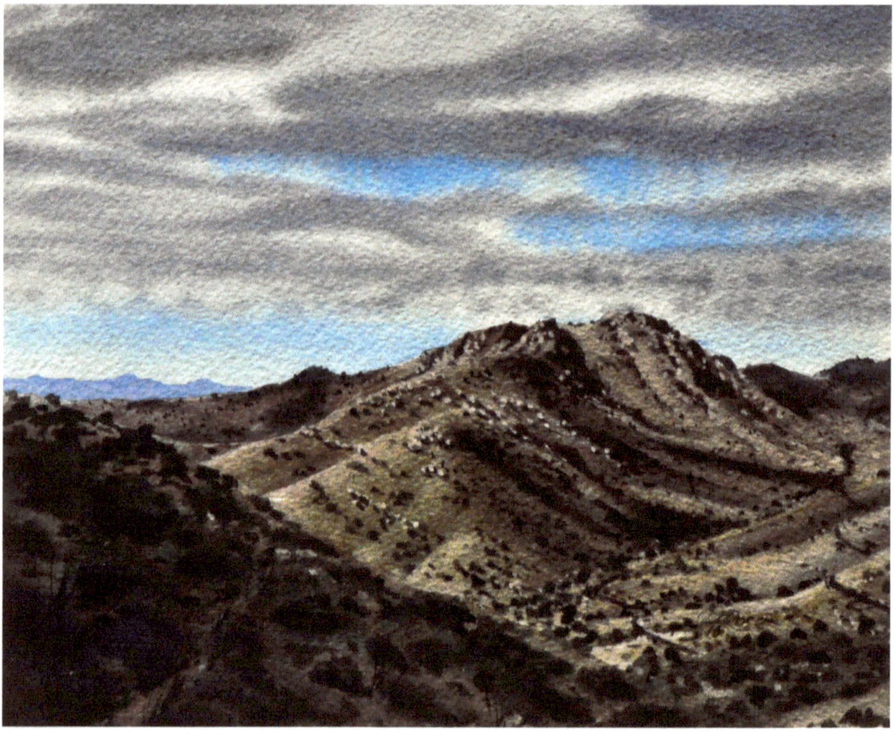

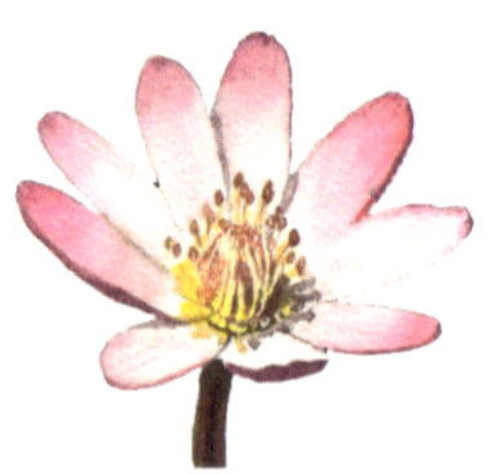

4. MOLINO BASIN

When I was photographing wildflowers for the book: "Mountain Wildflowers" I hiked a three and a half mile loop in Molino Basin once a week for a year. Altogether I found over three hundred different flowering species. Any year when there are good Winter rains, many Spring flowers appear.

The Arizona Trail runs through Molino Basin. It reaches this basin from the Rincon Mountains, going over Agua Caliente Hill, then descending into a valley and after that climbing a saddle from which one can see the whole of Molino Basin. This picture shows the view from that saddle. The trail then drops down into the basin, and continues on to Gordon Hirabayashi camp ground.

Desert Anemone
Anemone tuberosa

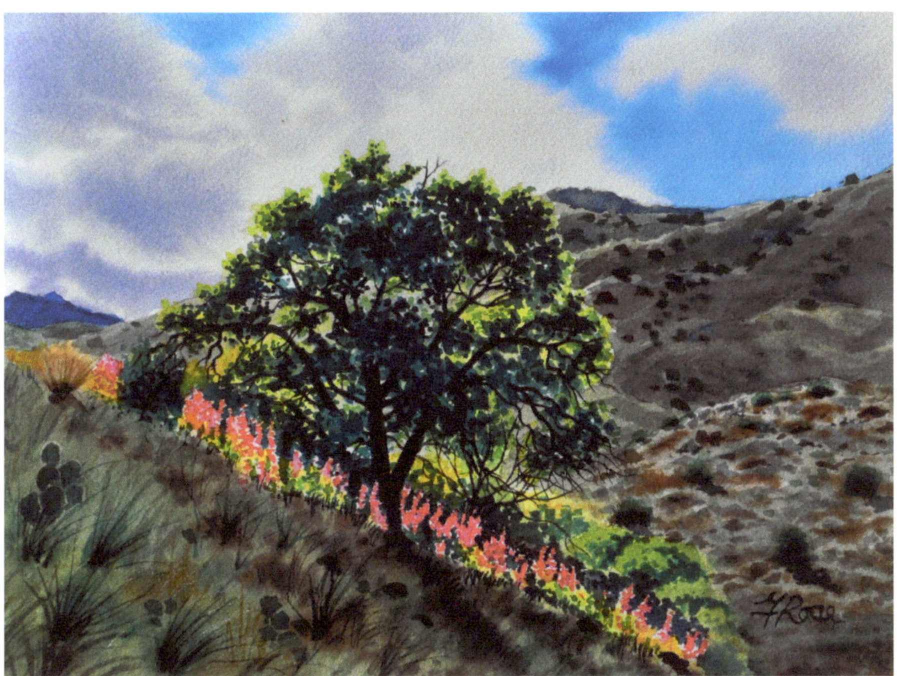

The lowest camp site in this range is in this basin. *Molino* is Spanish for *Mill*. During the construction of the highway, there were active mines in this valley, with their own mill, and so they gave it the name *Molino Basin*. The campground is closed in the hot summer months, but is always open to hikers.

There is not much to see during the Summer months until the monsoon rains. This brings new life to the basin with plants blooming well into the Fall and early Winter.

This oak tree shelters lots of Mohave Beardtongue in the Spring.

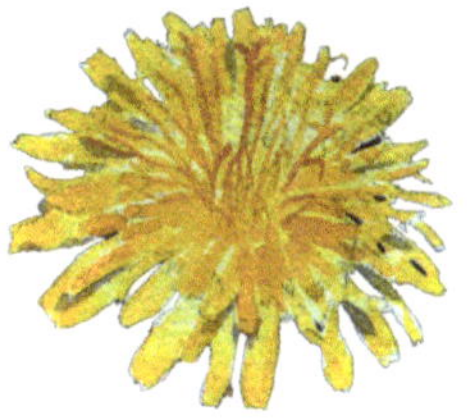

Dandelion
Taraxacum officinale

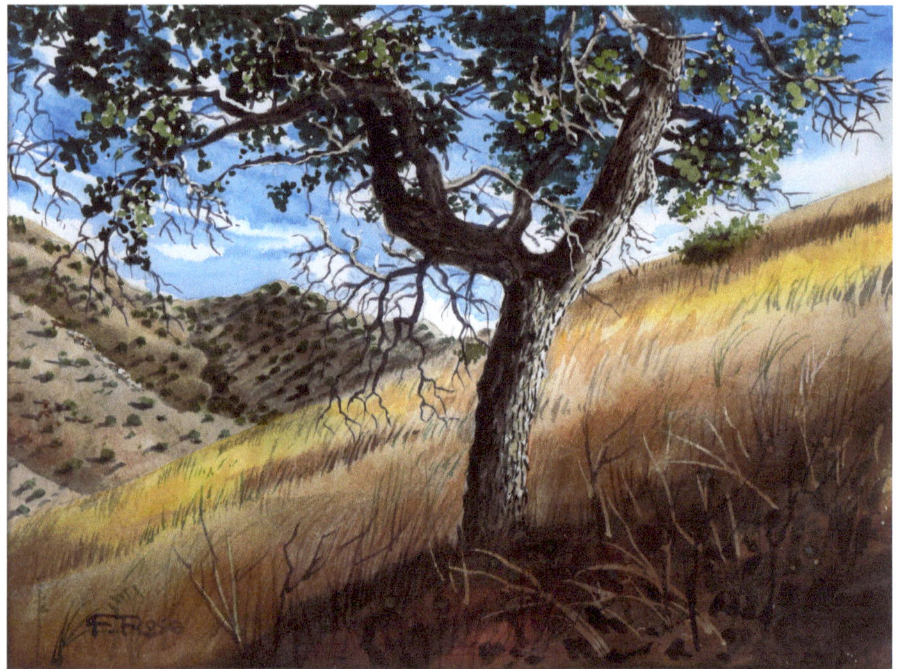

There is a paved road in Molino Basin with a number of campsites. I sometimes hike to the top of the road, and then take a short trail that connects with the Arizona trail. I turn left on this trail to make my way back to the car park.

At the high point of the trail there is this attractive Mexican Blue Oak. I call this place "Snack-Rock" because it is a good place to stop and enjoy the view.

From here the trail drops down to connect with the camp road, which you can then follow back to the parking lot.

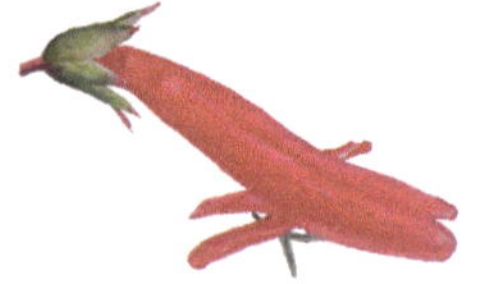

Bearded Penstemon
Penstemon barbatus

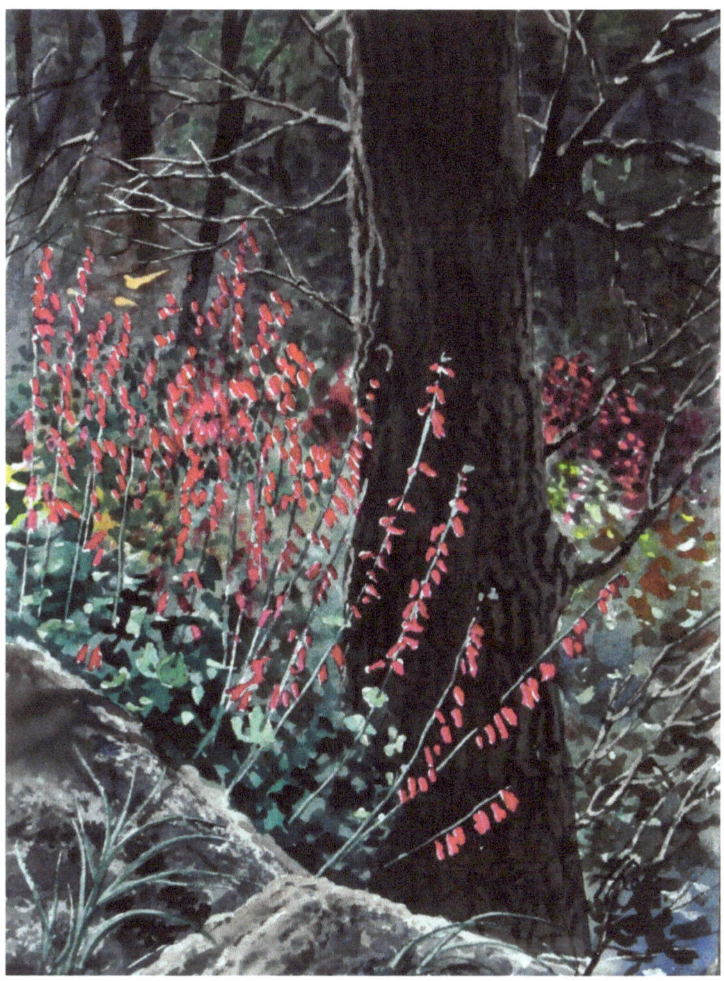

After a reasonably wet winter, there are many flowers blooming in Molino Basin. One of my favorites is Mohave Beardtongue, seen here under an oak tree. It seems to enjoy the shade.

The whole area is quite charming, and when I am there, although less than a half hour away from Tucson, I feel as if I am in another world. It is usually cool and the only sounds are of rustling leaves and thin streams of water tumbling over the rocks.If I sit still eventually I notice tiny wildflowers, insects, birds and other living things that call this home.

Mohave Beardtongue
Penstemon pseudospectabilis

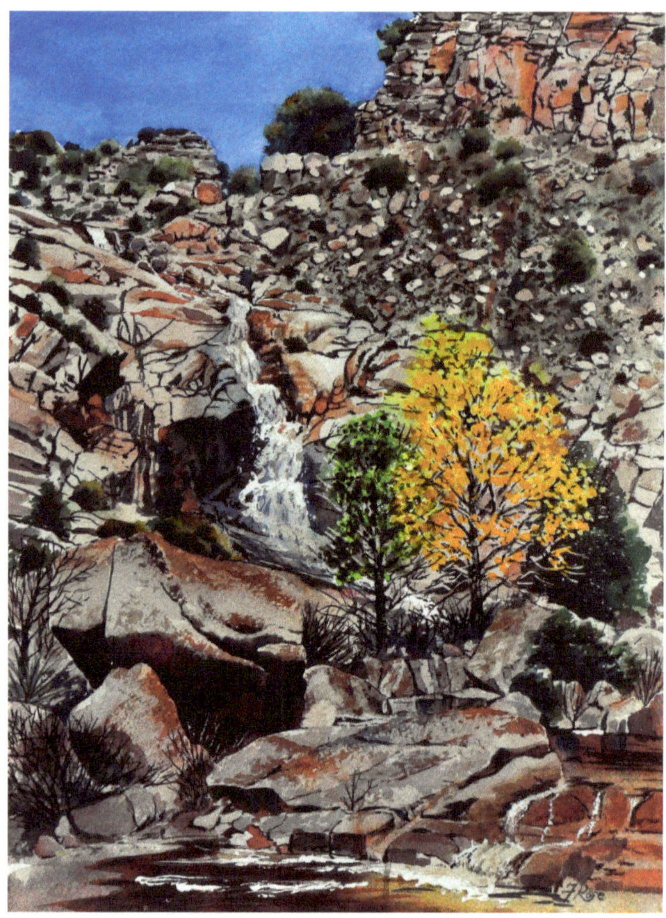

Once I was hiking up to Bellota Saddle, and stopped to catch my breath. Looking below me I noticed a trail far below going off to the right, that seemed to follow the stream. Later I was able to make a special trip to follow this unnamed and unmarked trail. After running parallel to the stream bed more or less, it drops down to a crossing. On the other side of the gully there is a faint trail leading up a hill. The beginning of the trail is fairly steep, then levels off somewhat. After rounding a bend I suddenly came on the falls. I call them "Molino Falls" though I have never seen that name used on any map. The trail comes to the middle of the cascade. It is possible to continue up even to the top of the falls, or descend to a flat area at the bottom, where this painting was done. There are some cottonwood trees growing in this stretch, and, on a far cliff a saguaro surviving about 4800 feet in elevation.

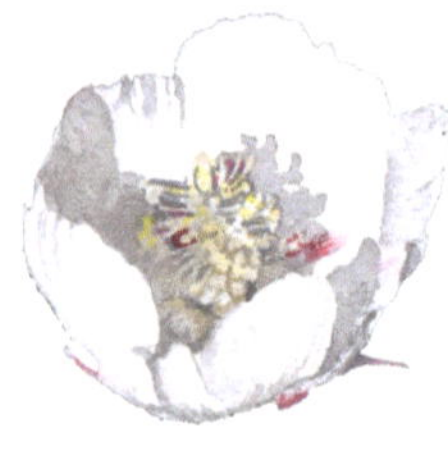

Desert Cotton
Gossypium thurberi

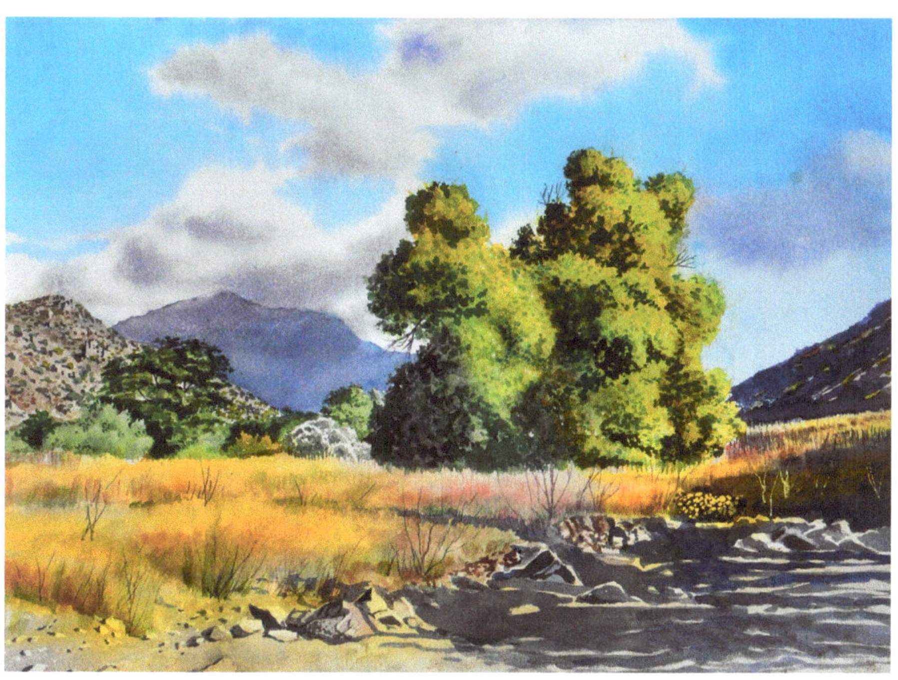

5. GORDON HIRABAYASHI

When we moved to Tucson in 1982 this was called "Prison Camp". The Hitchcock Highway, was started in 1933 using prison labor. After the first seven miles were built, a camp was established for the prisoners. It was an honor camp, with no walls or fence. After the road was finished in 1950 , the camp was used for other purposes, being finally demolished in the 1970s.

The Arizona Trail runs through the area and there is parking for cars and horses. In this picture we see something of the cottonwood trees that line the stream bed running through the camp.

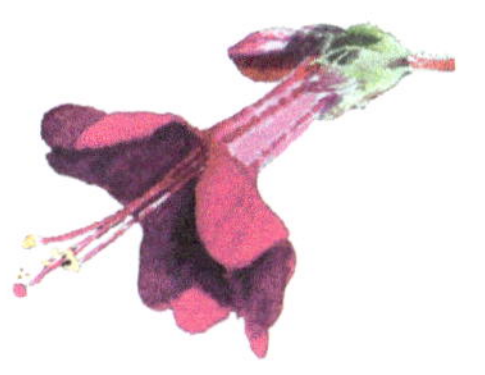

Scarlet Four O'clock
Mirabilis coccinea

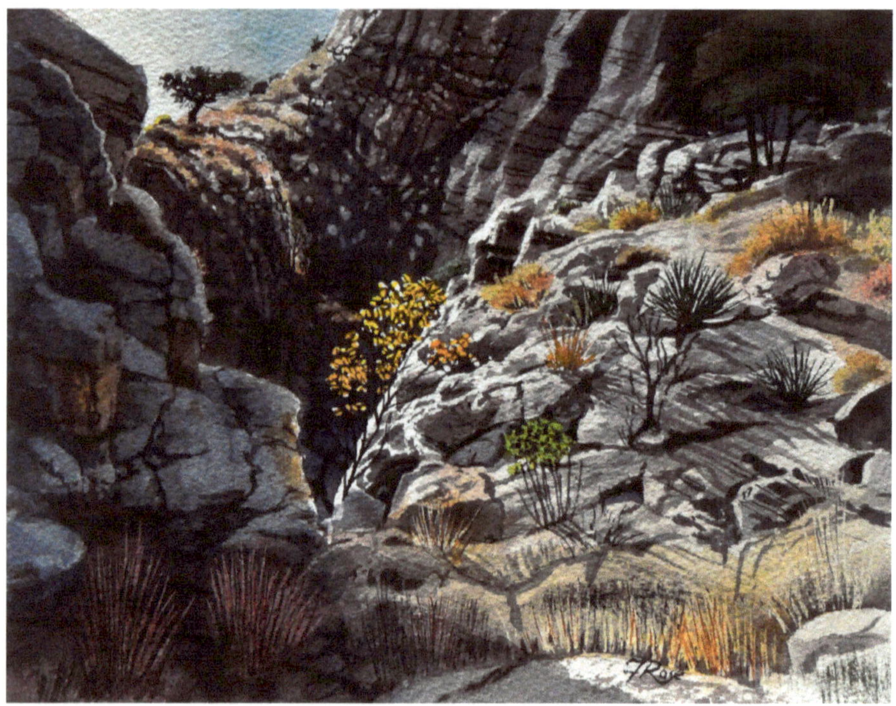

Going through the old Prison Camp area you can take the trail toward
Sycamore reservoir. Instead of following the main trail, turn left
and follow the stream bed. Eventually you will come to the top of a
waterfall. There is a route down to the bottom of the falls. This is a
rock climbing area. Thinking that I was alone, I have at times been
startled to hear voices below me and on the distant rock faces.

The tree with yellow leaves in the lower middle part of the painting,
seemingly growing out of the rocks, was not there when I returned a
year later, having been washed out by the heavy rains.

The tree on the ridge is probably a Mexican Blue Oak.

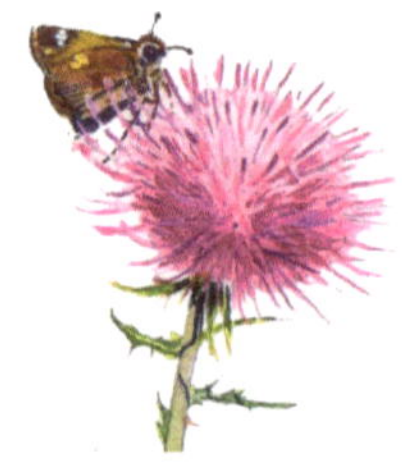

New Mexico Thistle
Cirsium neomexicanum

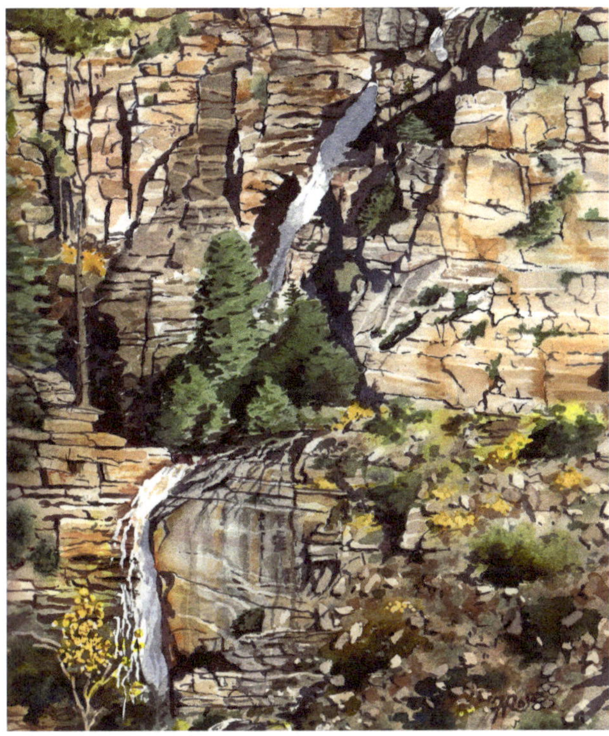

6. SEVEN CATARACTS

Very soon after arriving in Arizona in 1982, my wife and I bought
a copy of a "Trail Guide to the Santa Catalina Mountains" by Eber
Glendening and Pete Cowgill. Our copy soon became threadbare as we
took it on our mountain hikes year after year.

About this area between mile posts 9 and 10, they wrote: "These
specacular falls, or cataracts when running are easily seen from the
General Hitchcock highway." They go on to say: "The falls vary in
height from twenty to nearly one hundred feet with a pool at the one
being large enought to swim in."(p. 116)

We often found ourselves stopping to look at the falls, especially in
the rainy season, and I have made a number of attempts to catch their
special beauty in watercolors. On one occasion we took our visiting
family here, only to find that we were in the midst of
a thick cloud. We could hear the roar of the falls but
could not see this beautiful feature of the mountains.
When they widened the road (1988-2005) they
enlarged the parking area and built a wall for people
to lean on while enjoying the falls. Below it there is
a Springtime shrub called "Fendlerbush" with its
beautiful white flowers.

Fendlerbush
Fendlera wrightii

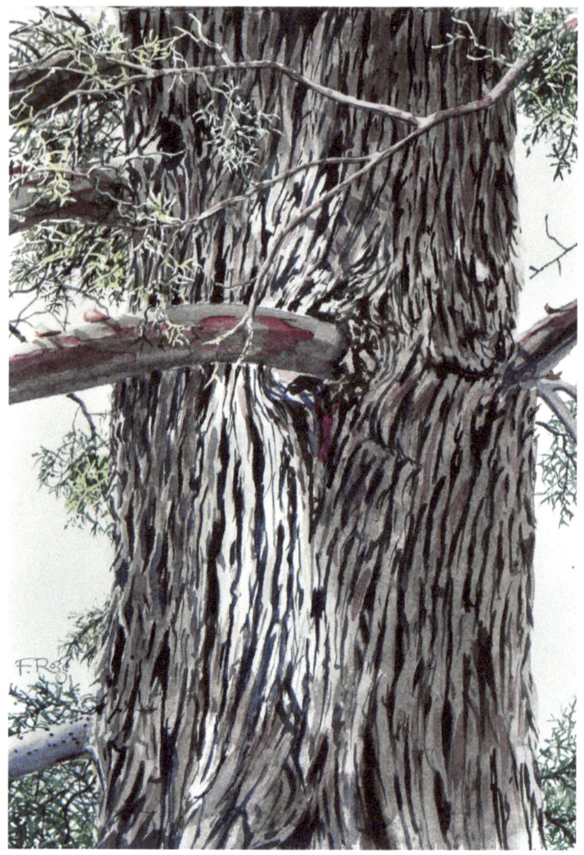

7. BEAR CANYON

The Bear Canyon Creek starts between Green Mountain and Guthrie Mountain. It flows down through the Hitchcock camp ground, crosses under the road through the Chihuahua Pine picnic area, crosses again through Middle Bear, and, from the Cypress picnic area follows the highway for two miles. This is a rich riparian zone with an Arizona Cypress that is over 100 feet tall (sometimes called "Big Cy"), near the middle. It then descends through the Sycamore reservoir, and to the East of Thimble Peak.

There are three picnic areas here. Going up the mountain they are: Cypress, Middle Bear (both on your right) and Chihuahua Pine (on your left). This is a favorite destination for summer outings.

Just past the Middle Bear parking lot there is parking for the Green Mountain Trail and the Bug Spring Trail.

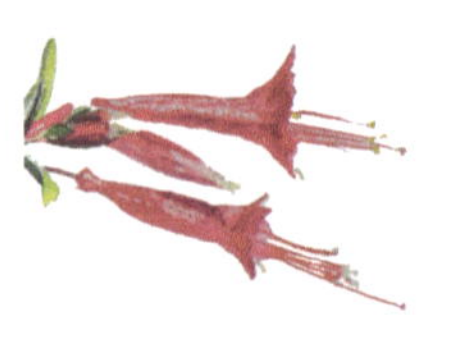

Hummingbird Trumpet
Epilobium canum

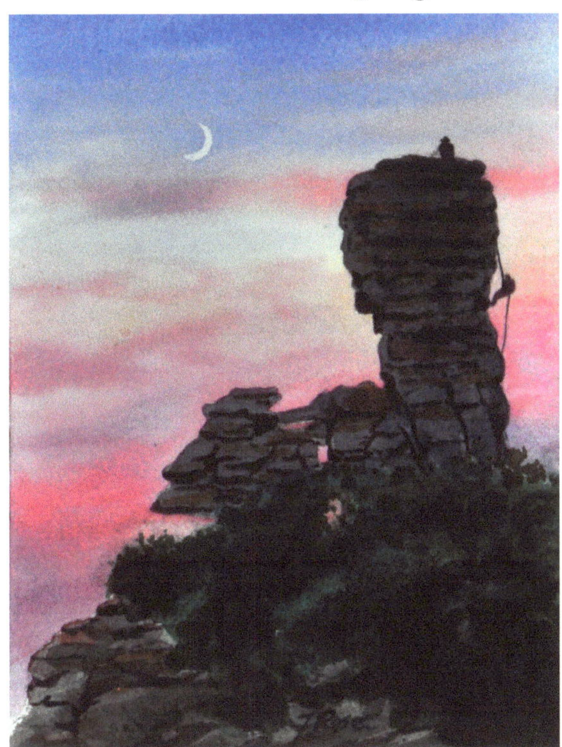

8. WINDY POINT VISTA

From the Hitchcock campground at the upper end of Bear Canyon there is a two mile stretch of road with views to the South, ending at Windy Point. The road improvements greatly expanded the number of parking places. On a week end summer evening every parking spot is full. Many come here to watch the sunset. There is a lookout rock with a guard rail where you can take in the whole basin surrounded by the Rincon Mountains, Santa Ritas directly south, and the Tucson Mountains to the West.

As you approach Windy Point you will see a Hoodoo on the right. It is not unusual to be startled by the sight of rock climbers scaling this formation.

Just below the rock overhang on the lower left side of this painting, there is a plaque to the man who was instrumental in getting the road built.

HONORABLE
FRANK HARRIS HITCHCOCK
THIS BEAUTIFUL HIGHWAY
WAS MADE POSSIBLE BY
HIS SINCERE INTEREST
AND UNCEASING EFFORTS.
IT IS DEDICATED TO
HIM AND SHALL BE
KNOWN AS
"HITCHCOCK HIGHWAY"

Fragrant Snakeroot
Ageratina herbacea

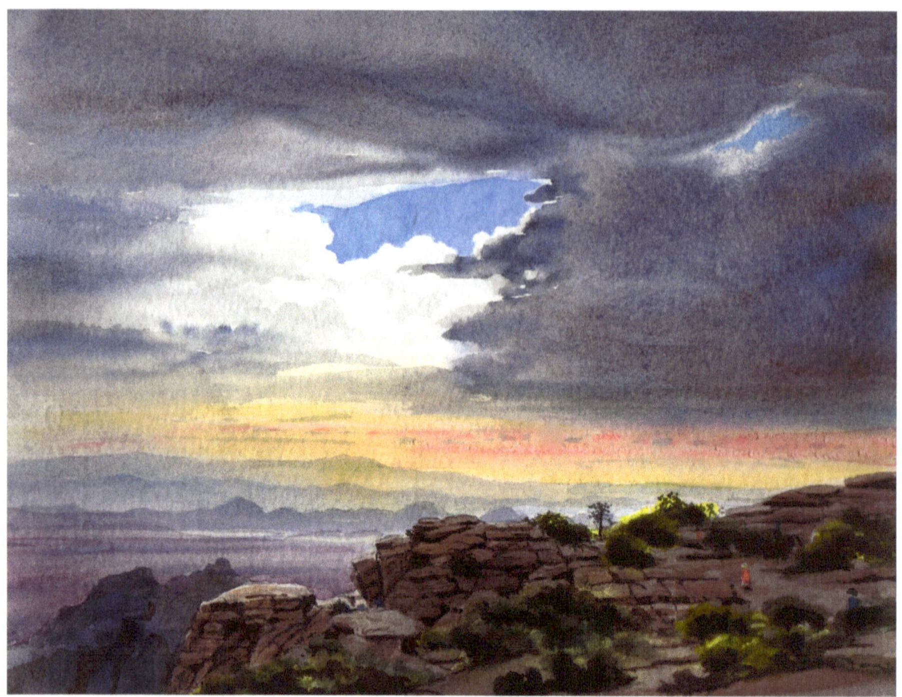

Windy Point Vista commands a panoramic view of the whole Tucson valley. In the far distance you can see part of the Tucson mountains, beyond which are Old Tucson movie set, and the Arizona Sonoran Desert Museum. A little to the left of that you might be able to see Kitt Peak, and further left, the triangular shaped Baboquivari Peak.

Due South you can make out the peaks of the Santa Rita mountains, beyond which you see almost to Mexico. To your left are the Rincon mountains.

A plaque in the parking lot shows that the road was improved from 1988 to July 6, 2005.

The overlook has a protective fence and signage telling about the view. People can walk past the washrooms, to explore the landscape and enjoy the sunset.

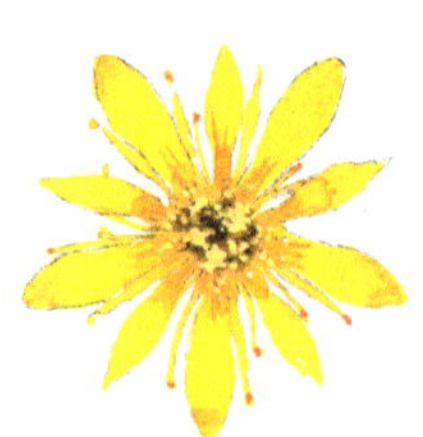

Blazing Star
Mentzelia multiflora

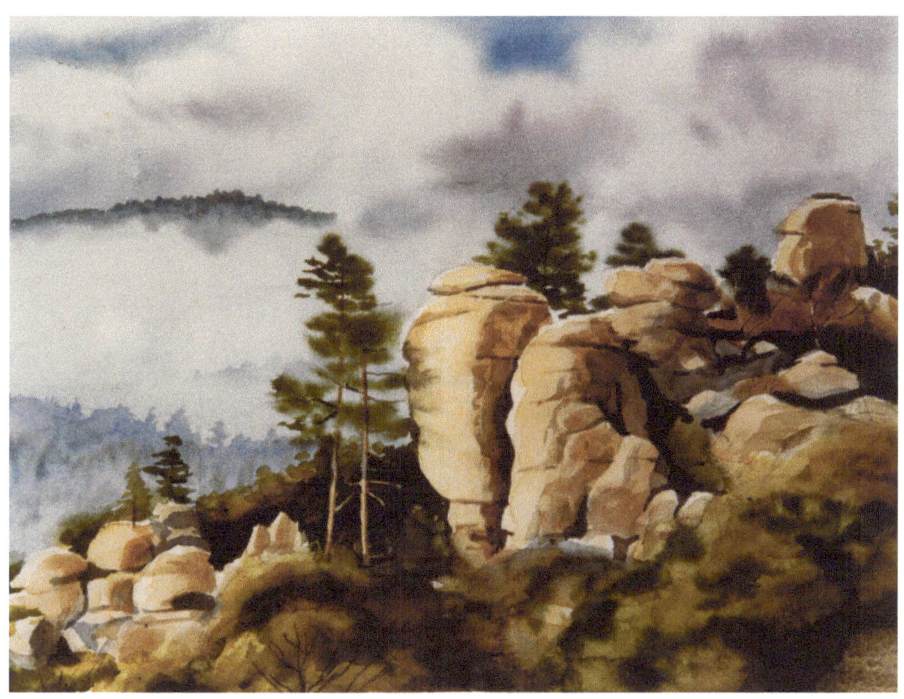

9. GEOLOGY VISTA POINT

Soon after Windy Point you come to a pull-off on the right called "Geology Vista". From this vantage point you can see Dos Cabezas, the mountain range just south of Wilcox 60 miles away.

Along the highway straight ahead of you are a number of the rock formations called "Hoodoos". These begin as fairly angular blocks that over time develop rounded edges. The Chiricahua Mountains, which you can see to the East and South, have a wonderful collection in Echo Canyon. The group in this painting is across the road from Geology Vista.

Life zones on the mountain range are listed on a sign at Geology Vista as:
3000' Sonoran Desert
4000' Semi-Desert Grasslands
5000' Oak Woodland and Chaparral
6000' Pine-Oak Woodland
7000' Ponderosa Pine Forest
8000' Mixed Conifer Forest.

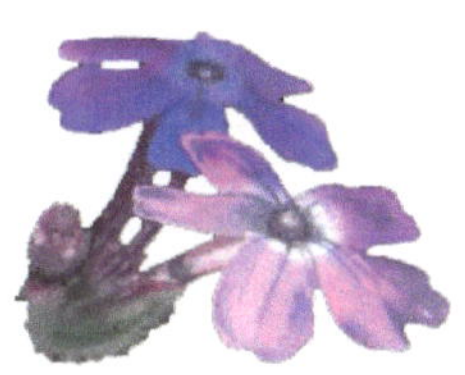

Goodding Verbena
Glandularia goodingii

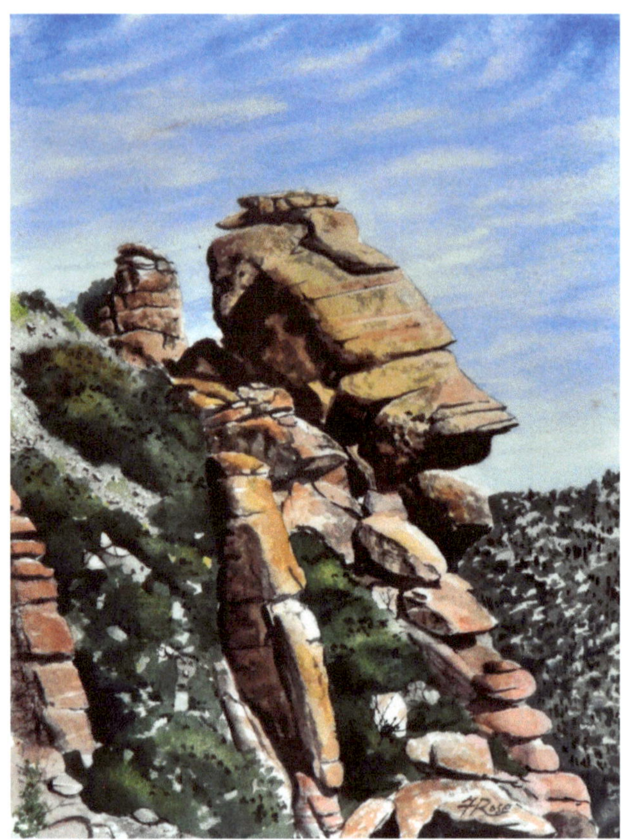

Perhaps the most dramatic of the Hoodoos is on the right as you drive past Geology Vista. It has been called a Goose, Duck, or a Knight in Shining Armor. Feel free to make up your own names for these strange and wonderful formations. Hoodoo is like the word Hobgoblin.

Soon after passing this rock formation, you head into the forest with no more views of the Tucson valley. Now you are surrounded by pine trees and other species giving you the feeling that you have arrived in a Canadian forest.

At almost 7000 feet, the road rises and falls as it varies between seven and eight thousand feet. To get higher than that, you need to go through Ski Valley to the top of the mountain

Santa Catalina Indian
Paintbrush
Castilleja tenuiflora

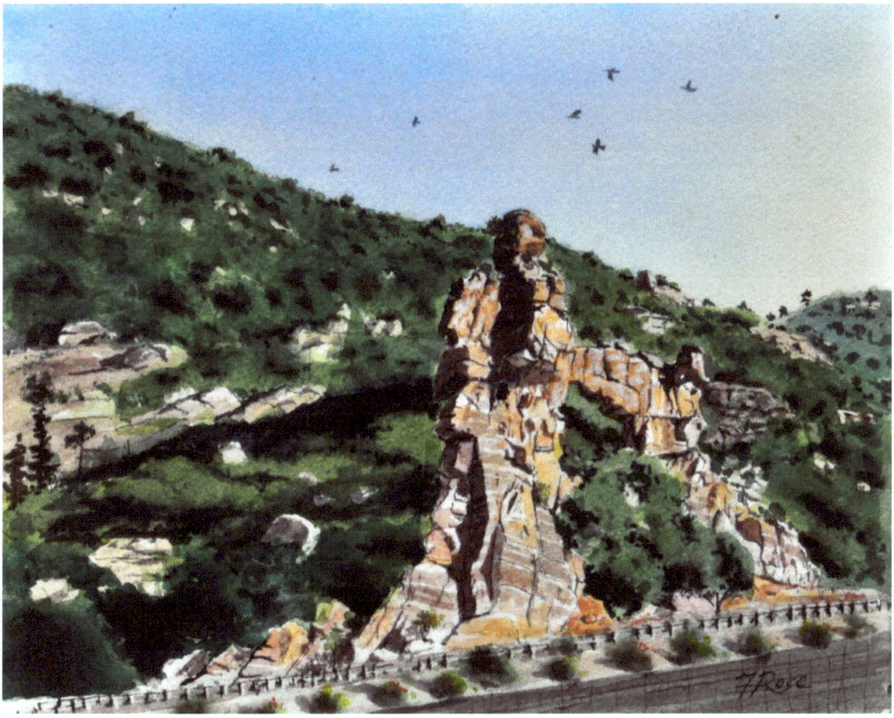

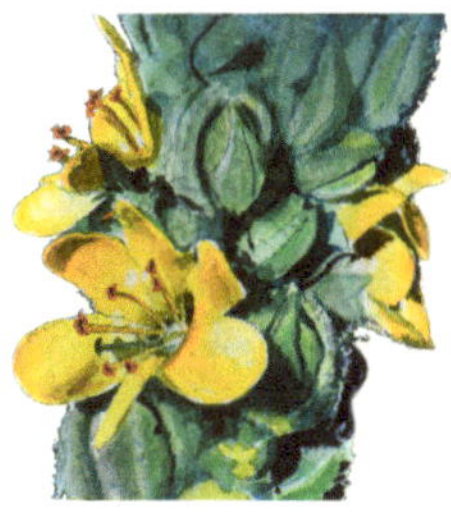

10. ROCK ARCH

Immediately after Mile Post 15, there is a pull off where you can look ahead and see a natural arch. The left side of the arch is a free-standing hoodoo. Though in this picture it looks very near the arch itself, there is quite a gap between the two.

During the rebuilding of the mountain highway many of us were concerned that the formation might topple. Luckily care was taken to preserve this dramatic feature.

Common Mullein
Verbascum thapsus

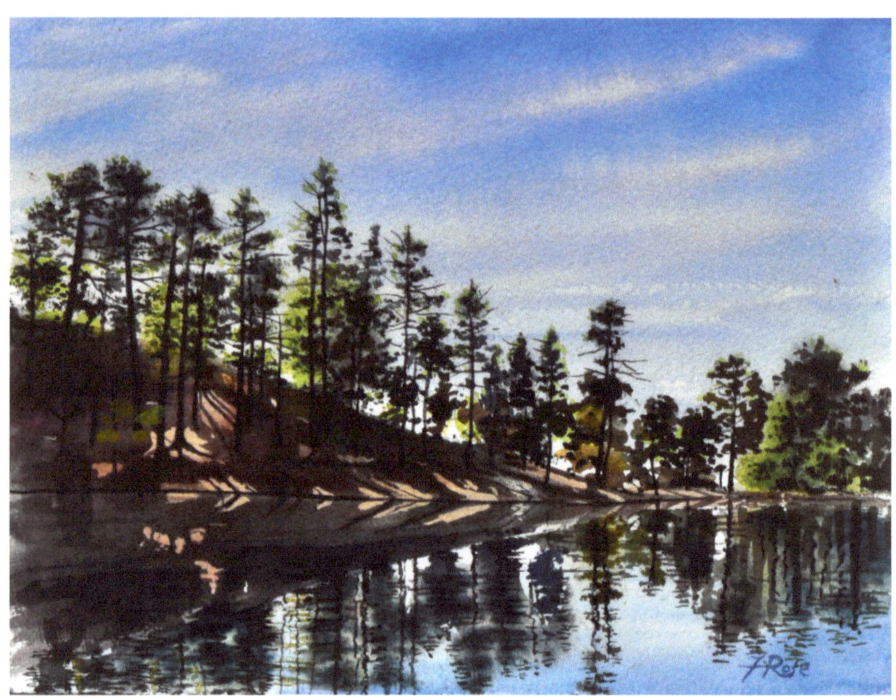

11. ROSE CANYON LAKE

Just before mile post 17 there is a road leading into Rose Canyon. This area is a private concession, so there is an extra fee for entering and camping. The seven acre lake is stocked with trout for fishing but, alas, no swimming. There is a special beauty and tranquillity at this solitary lake in the Catalinas.

This painting shows the lake in the winter, when the road is closed to cars. My friend and I walked over a mile to get to the lake to take photographs and were surprised to find that we were not the only people there. A couple of fishermen enjoyed the stillness with us.

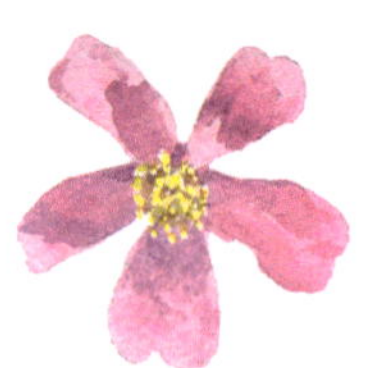

It is a very beautiful spot, with trails on either side of the lake and many camp sites along the road leading to the lake.

Arizona Rose
Rosa woodsii

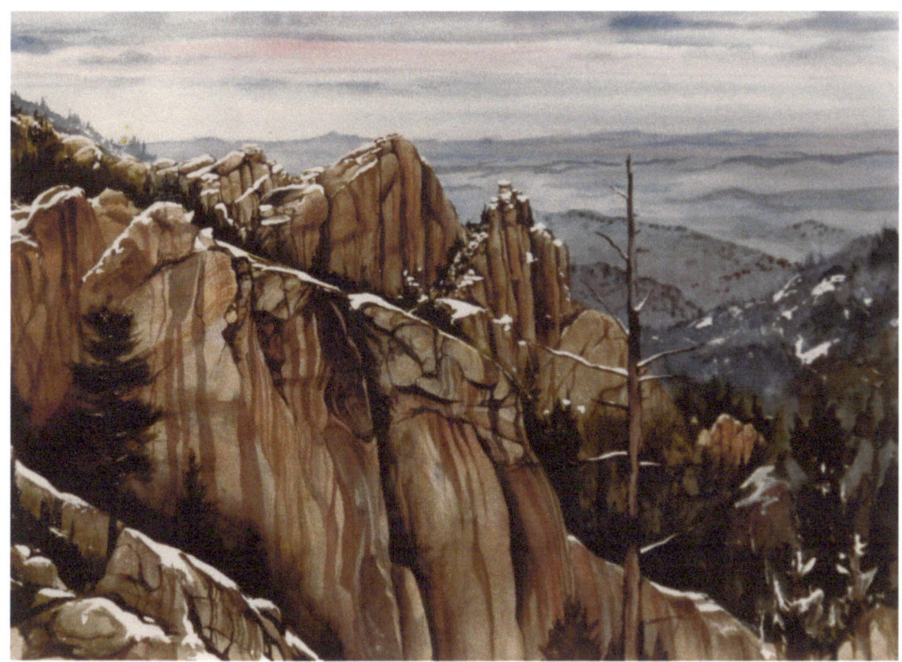

12. SAN PEDRO VISTA

Just a little past the entrance to Rose Canyon Lake there is trail-head parking for the Green Mountain Trail (which connects with the Hitchcock campground in Bear Canyon), and a short distance beyond that is San Pedro Vista.

This painting gives an idea of the view to the left with patches of snow on the rocks, and streaks of color where rock varnish has accumlated over the years. Rock varnish is formed when airborn dust particles containing various minerals adhere to damp places on the rock.

Below you can see the valley of the San Pedro River, which begins life in Mexico and flows north past the Catalinas, joining up later with the Gila River that flows past Phoenix.

An alternative section of the Arizona Trail passes through here, connecting with Incinerator Trail and Butterfly Trail.

Mountain Marigold
Tagetes lemmoni

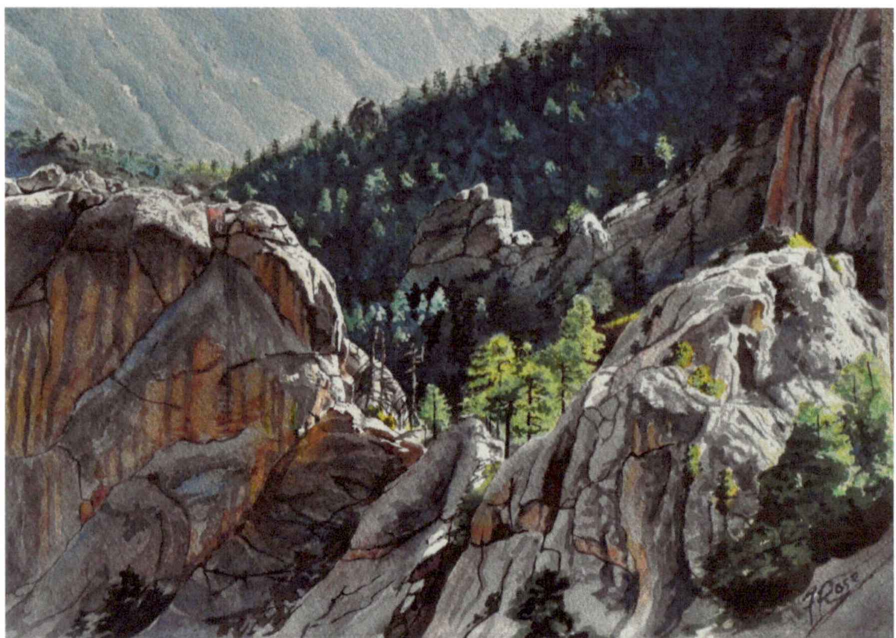

There are wonderful rock formations along this East face of the
Catalina mountains. In the distance you can see Mt. Graham, the
highest point in the Pinaleno Mountains, 10,720 feet.. On a clear day
it is possible to see the Mount Graham International Observatory, an
Astrophysical Research Site. This is the largest binocular telescope in
the world which began operations in 1993.

The Arizona Trail goes through the San Pedro Vista parking lot.
Hiking in the area to the right of this painting, you come to the largest
stand of Rusby's Primrose that I have seen in the range. It blooms
after the summer rains.

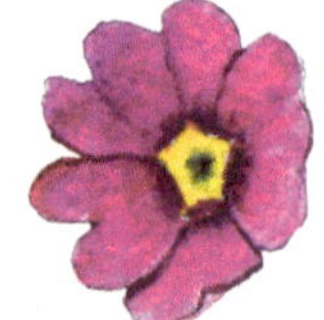

Ruby's Primrose
Primula rusbyi

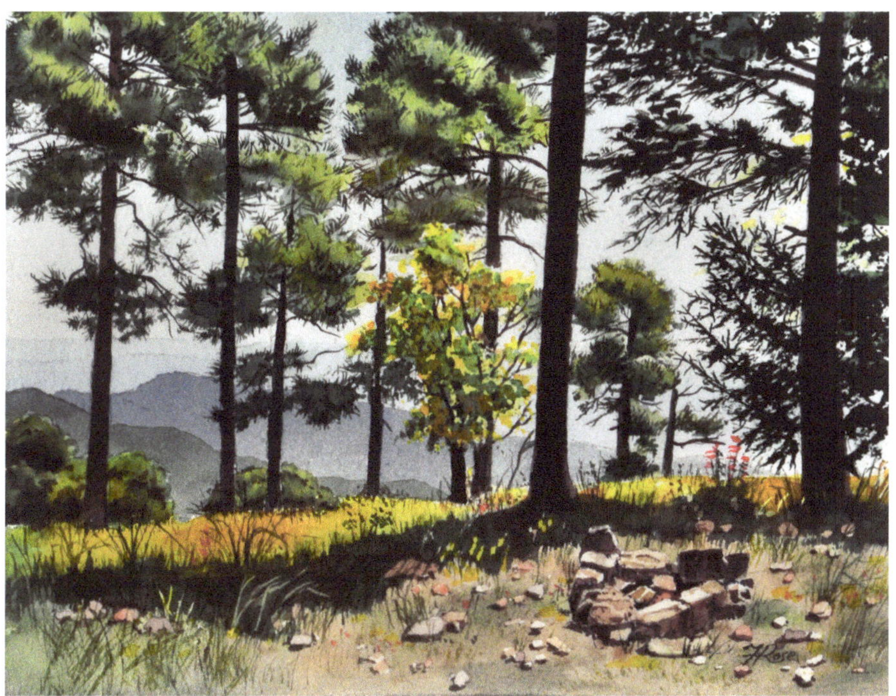

13. INCINERATOR RIDGE

Years ago a large incinerator was built so that the mountain residents could burn their trash. Incinerator Ridge Road takes you to the ridge where it was located. There is an area for parking and a trail. If you turn left, the trail will take you to Mt. Bigelow. If you follow the trail to the right you will see spectacular views on both sides. After dipping steeply down, the trail rises to Incinerator Peak (overlooking San Pedro Vista), with wonderful views on all sides. This peak was formerly known as Peck Basin Overlook.

It is particularly noticeable that there are many more trees on the north than on the south slopes of this ridge

This painting shows the view looking north to Oracle Ridge and the town of Oracle with its adjoining Oracle State Park.

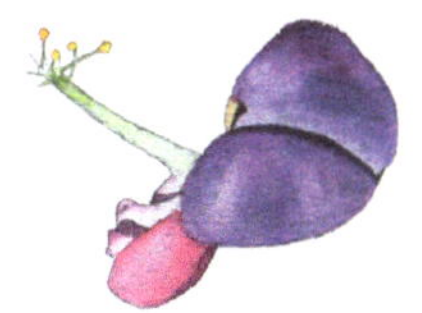

Long-leaf Cologania
Cologania angustifolia

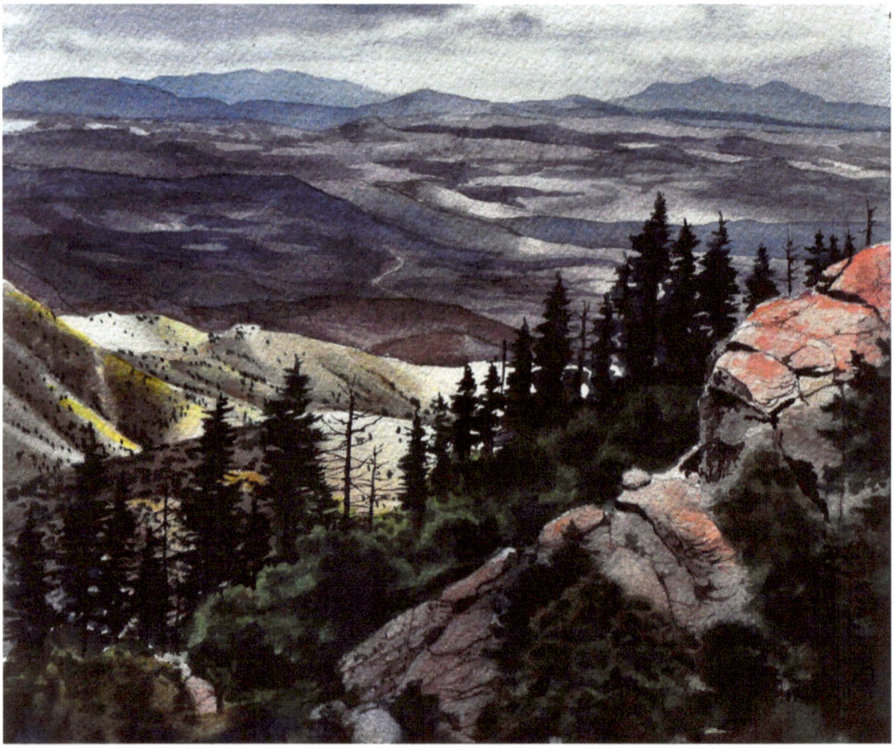

The Incinerator Ridge trail opens up to views of the North. When we first moved to Tucson the little town of San Manuel still had its smelter, and tall brick tower. Aravaipa canyon, Winkelman and Globe are all off in the distance. The San Pedro river flows through this valley, heading north to connect with the Gila River that goes to Phoenix and beyond.

This painting was done during the Monsoon season with heavy rains and dramatic lighting as shafts of sunlight broke through the cloud cover.

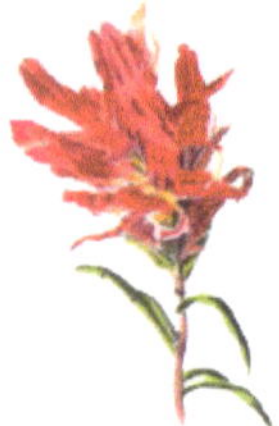

Rincon Mountain Indian
Paintbrush
Castilleja austromontana

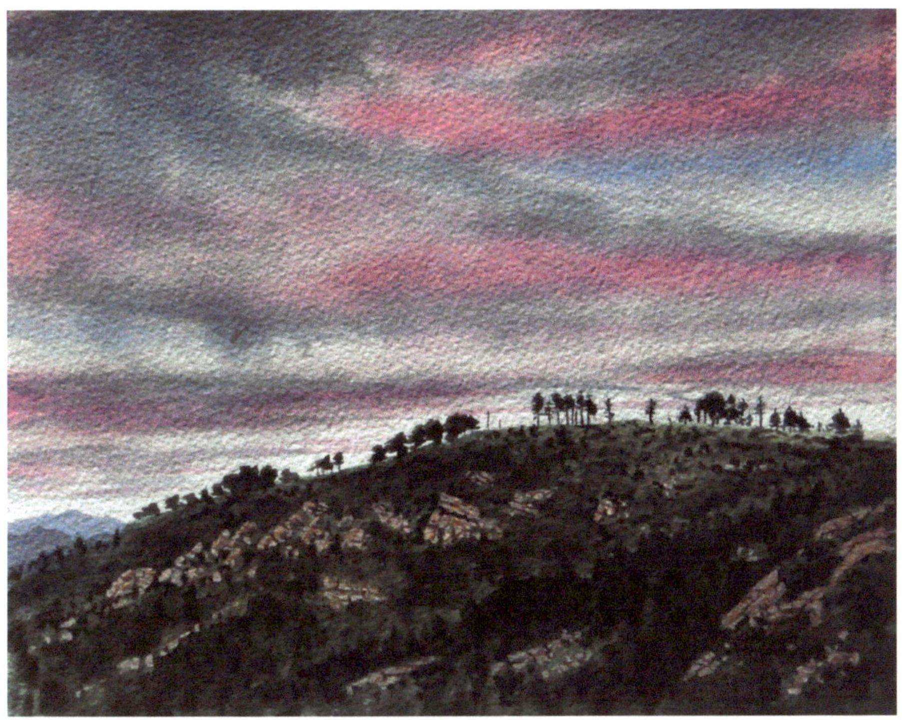

14. PALISADES TRAIL

This is one of the original pack trails. My wife, with her sister Ann, and I hiked down this trail to Sabino Canyon as part of our training to hike the Grand Canyon. We started in snow, and hiked down into the heat, exactly as we did in the Grand Canyon a few months later. It involved a drop of about 4000 feet in 8 miles.

Organization Ridge road is a turning left just before you reach the Palisades Ranger Station. There are a number of organizations with camp sites - The Boys and Girls Scouts, Baptists, Latter Day Saints, and a campground called Shower's Point, as well as the trailhead for the Palisades Trail.

Meadow Goat's-Beard
Tragopogon dubius

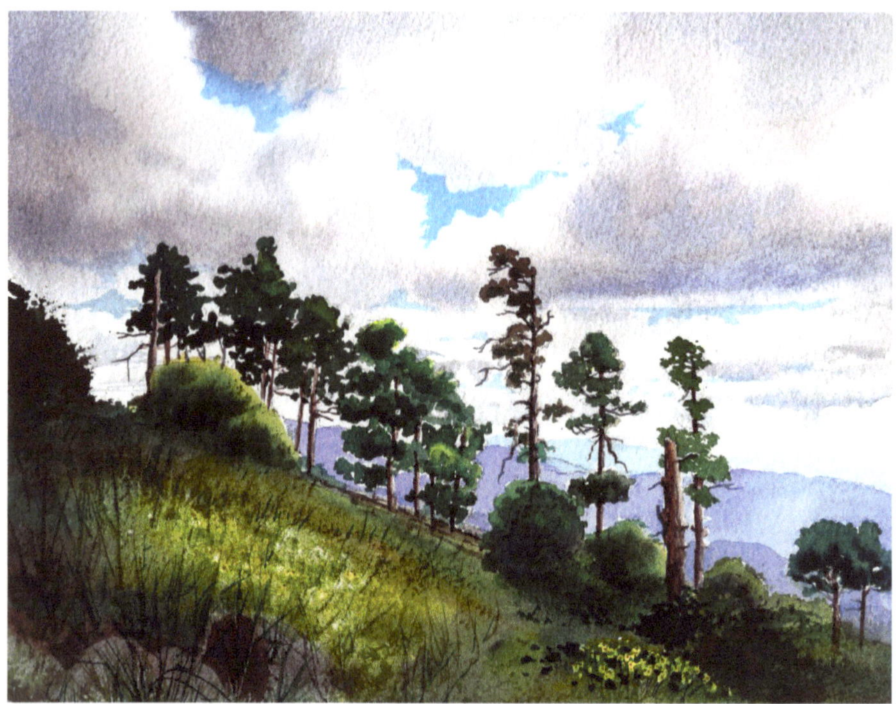

15. MOUNT BIGELOW

Mount Bigelow is the second highest peak in the range at 8550 feet. John Bigelow was a botanist with several plants on the mountain named after him. There is a dirt road going off to the right to the top of this mountain, with a connection to the Butterfly trail, and Knagge Trail (seldom used, since it drops down into the heat). Driving up the road you pass a rock face on your right just before you reach the top of Mount Bigelow, one of the most beautiful collection of wildflowers on the mountain.

Just below Mt. Bigelow there is a mostly-bare hill with views overlooking Tucson, the view to the right of this painting. In the distance you can see the Rincon Mountains.

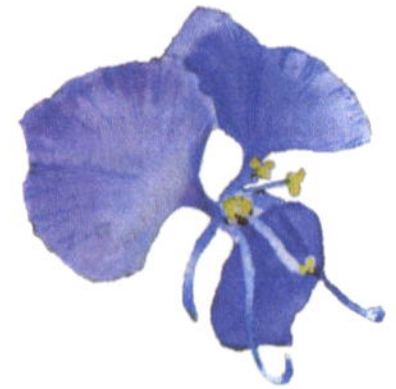

Dayflower
Commelina dianthifolia

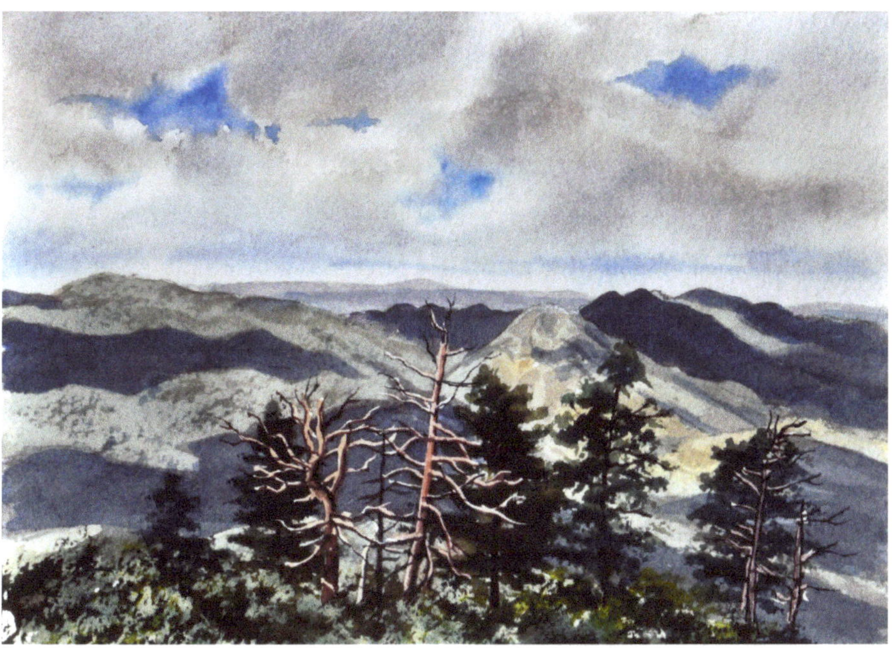

Often the high points on the mountains are in the clouds. I caught the view depicted in the painting above when we parked for a plant walk up the road to Mt. Bigelow. By the time we reached the parking lot at the top, the sun was out and we could see Oracle Ridge leading off into the distance in the North.

Beyond the ridge lies the town of Oracle and Oracle State park. The substrate is mostly sedimentary rocks, like limestone and sandstone, which supports a number of plants that are not found elsewhere in the range.

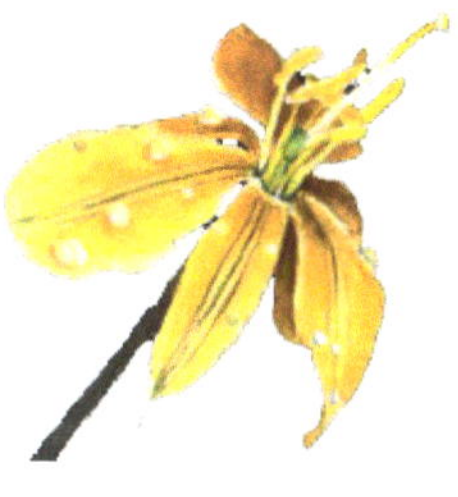

Torrey's Craglily
Echeandia flavescens

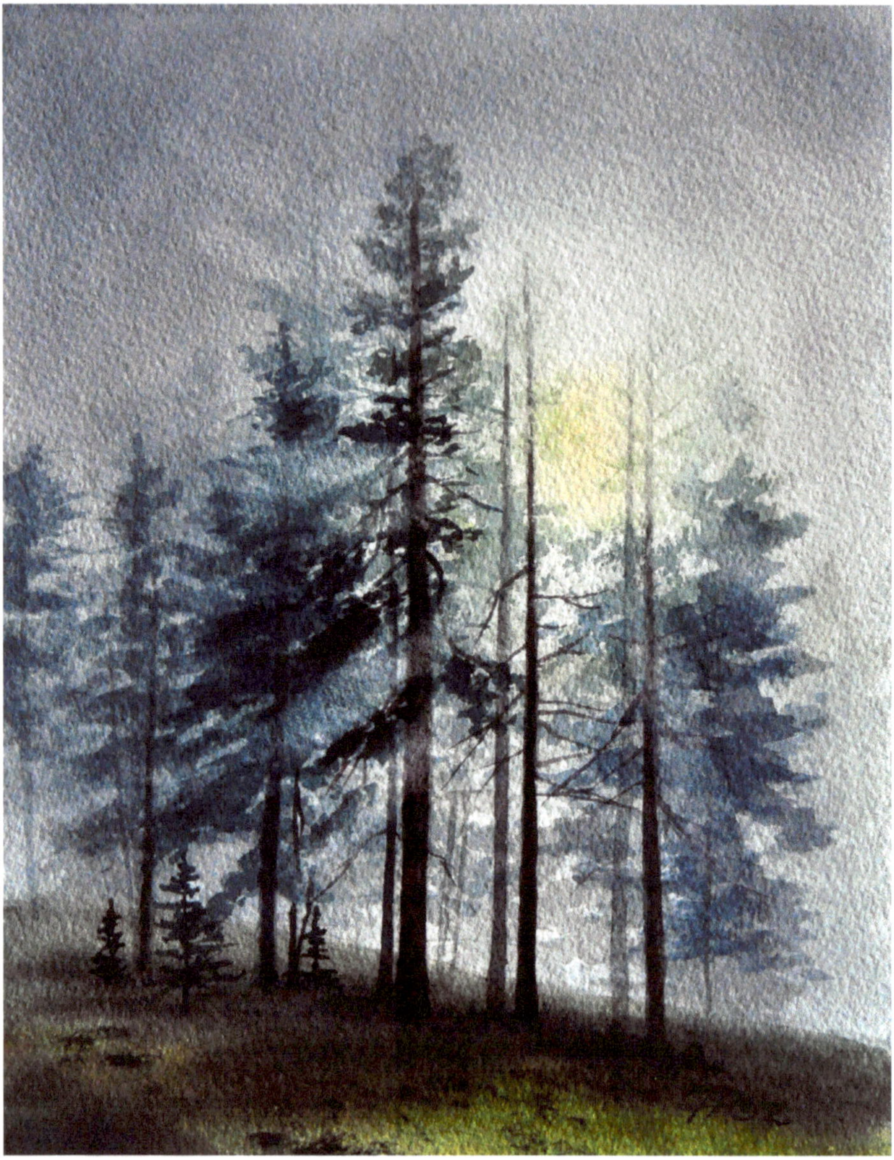

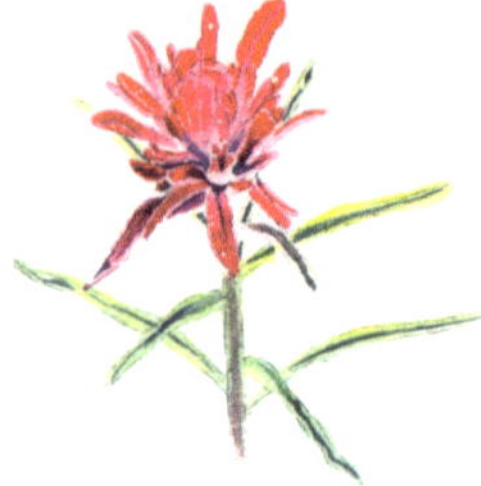

Wholeleaf Indian Paintbrush
   Castilleja integra

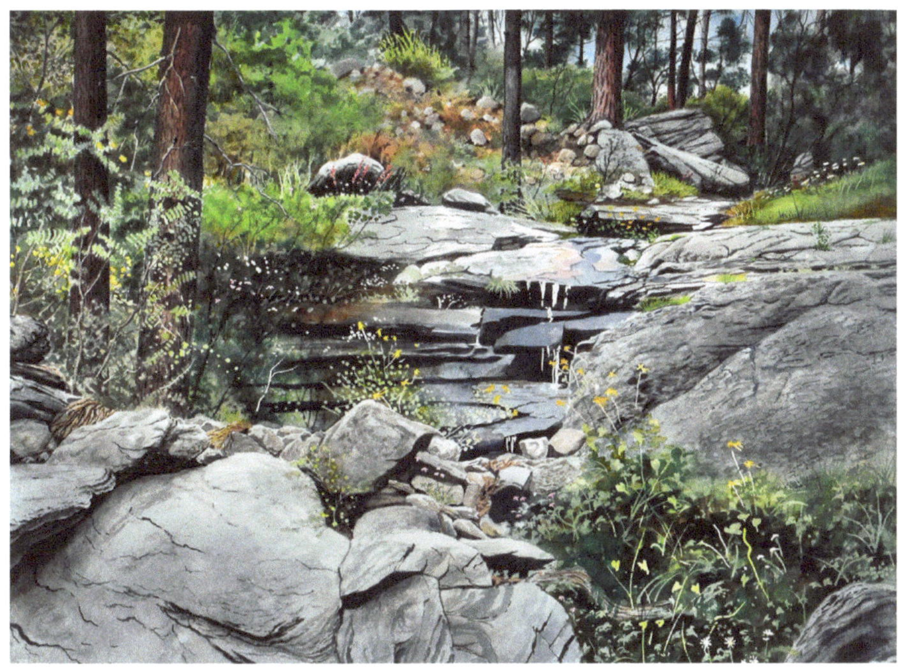

16. BOX CAMP TRAIL

This trail goes from the Hitchcock Highway down into the Tucson valley. After a brief rise, the path crosses under power lines, enters a rocky area, climbs a hill with commanding views to the left and the right, and then continues down the mountain. Where the stream crosses the trail Lobelia, Columbines and other beautiful flowers may be seen.

After just under five miles you come to Apache Spring. It is 7.1 miles to Sabino Basin and another two and a half miles to the top of Sabino Canyon. From there it is about 4 more miles to the visitor's center. Once it was the most popular packhorse route into the mountains.

Lots of wildflowers grow here, especially where the trail follows the creek.

Mahogany Milkweed
Asclepias hypoleuca

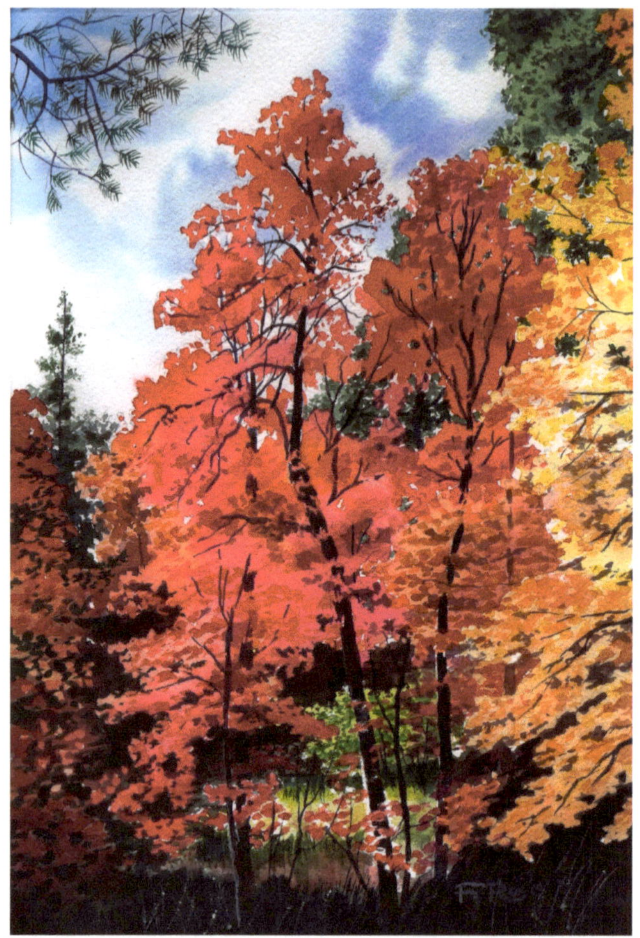

17. BEAR WALLOW

The highway takes a hairpin bend at mile post 22. At this point it is crossing Bear Wallow, and there is a very tall tunnel under the road, which I call the Giraffe Tunnel since it is high enough for even those animals to pass through. There is a path that runs through the tunnel. The lower end is at the parking lot for the Sunset Trail. The upper end crosses the Mt. Bigelow Road at a little meadow.

This is a wonderful place to see the Big Tooth maples in their Fall colors which range from yellow, through orange to a beautiful red.

Clubleaf Cinquefoil
Potentilla subviscosa

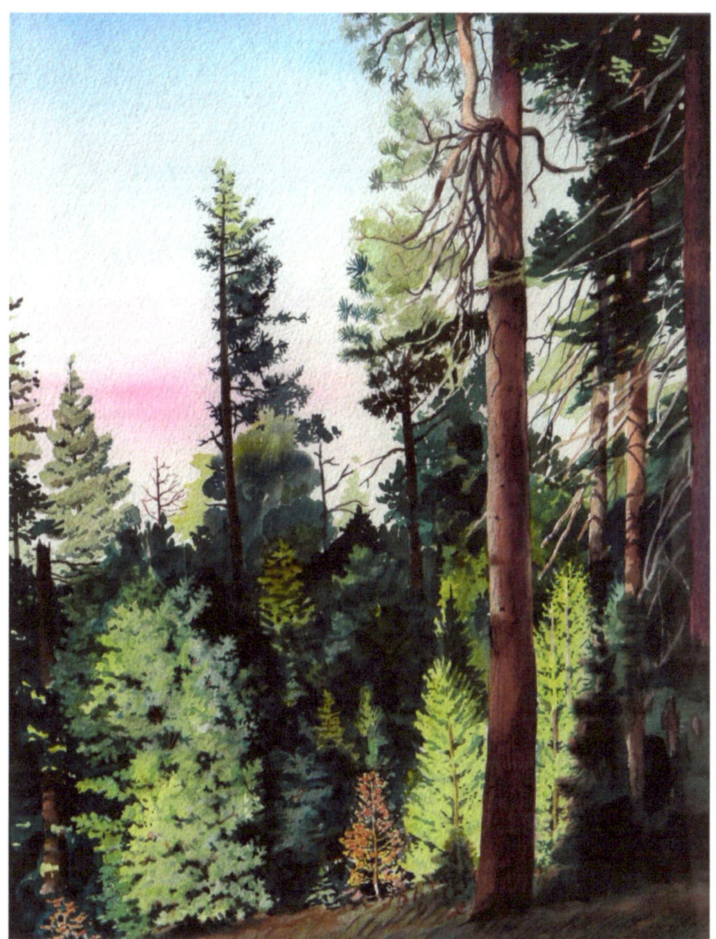

I have never seen a bear in these mountains, though there were scores of them in the past. Bears do not mix well with human populations, so over time any that become a nuisance are removed.

This is a point where Bear Wallow trail sort of ends, but you can cross the road and continue up to the first Observatory on the mountains, with its two telescopes. Its sign says: *University of Arizona Observatories, operated by Steward Observatories.*

Trees grow really well in this part of the range. They are considerably taller than those on the south-facing slopes, more resistant to fire, and more densely packed. There are a number of areas suitable for camping in this part of the range.

Arizona Valerian
Valeriana arizonica

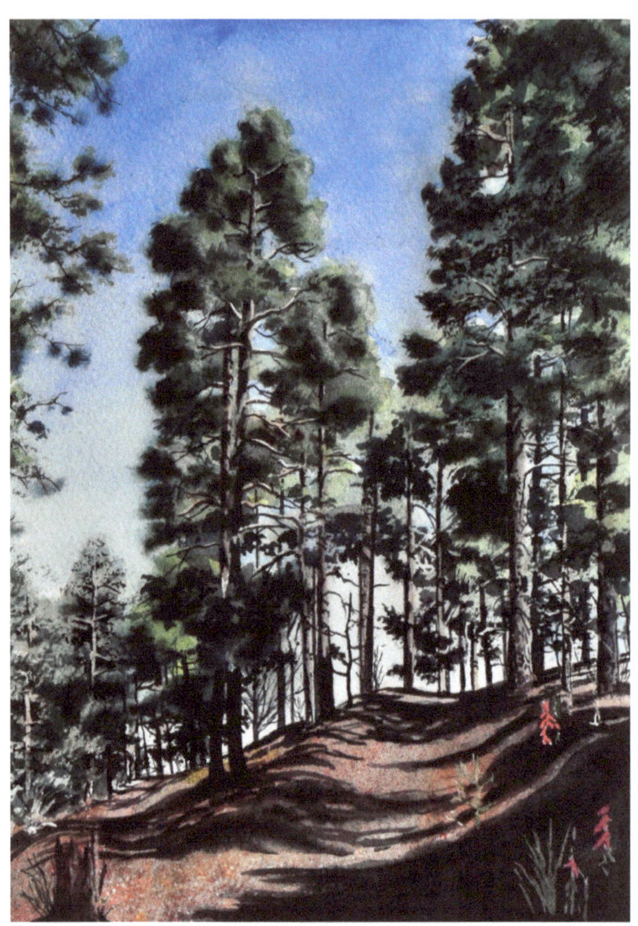

18. BUTTERFLY TRAIL

The Butterfly Trail has two ends. There is trail parking at the bathroom area on the right a short distance before you come to the Palisades Ranger Station. The trail rises to a saddle, and then drops steeply down on the north side of the mountain.
The West end of the trail is more or less opposite the parking for the Sunset Trail. The first part of the trail is a paved road, which turns into a dirt road, and, at the point shown in the painting, the road goes off to the right to a cabin, but the trail goes straight ahead, eventually dropping down the mountain. At the lowest point it gets near Novio Springs. The remains of a World War II airplane are still visible a short distance up a side trail. The whole trail is just under six miles long.

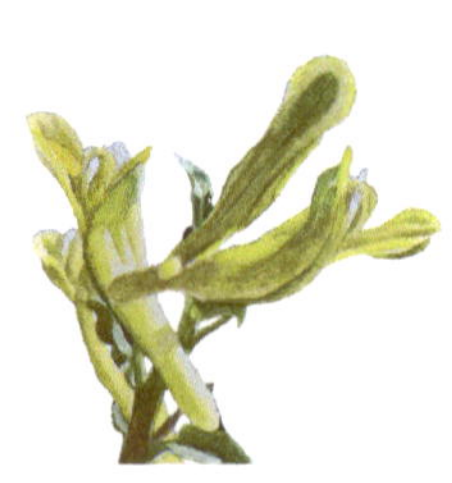

Golden Smoke
Corydalis aurea

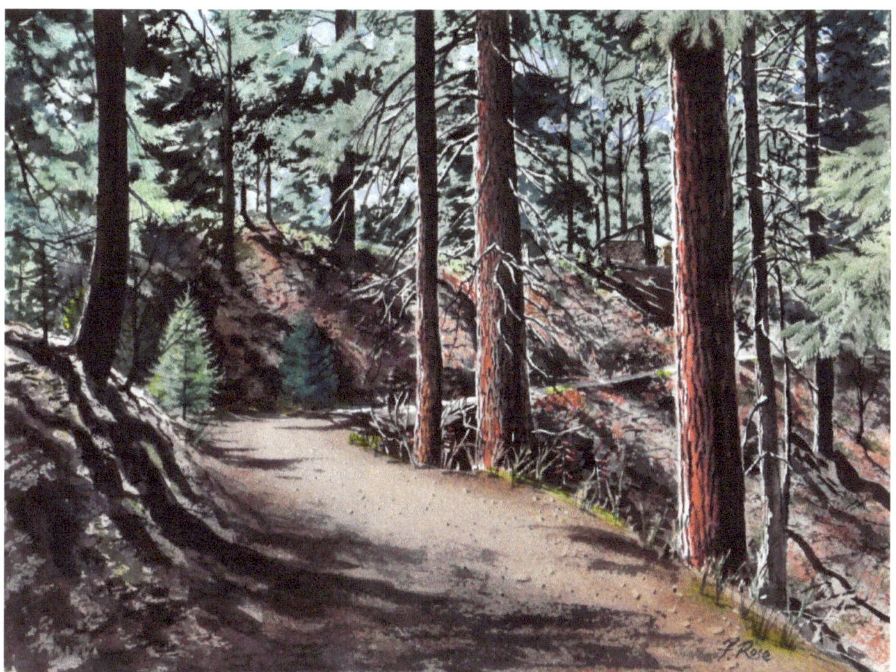

The previous painting shows the Butterfly Trail branching off from a camp road. When I took the photograph for that painting I turned around to see the view back to the trail-head parking. Those who hiked the Butterfly Trail from its East end will be relieved to see that their long slog up the mountain is finally over.

The bathroom building can be seen toward the right side of this painting.

Gaura
Gaura hexandra

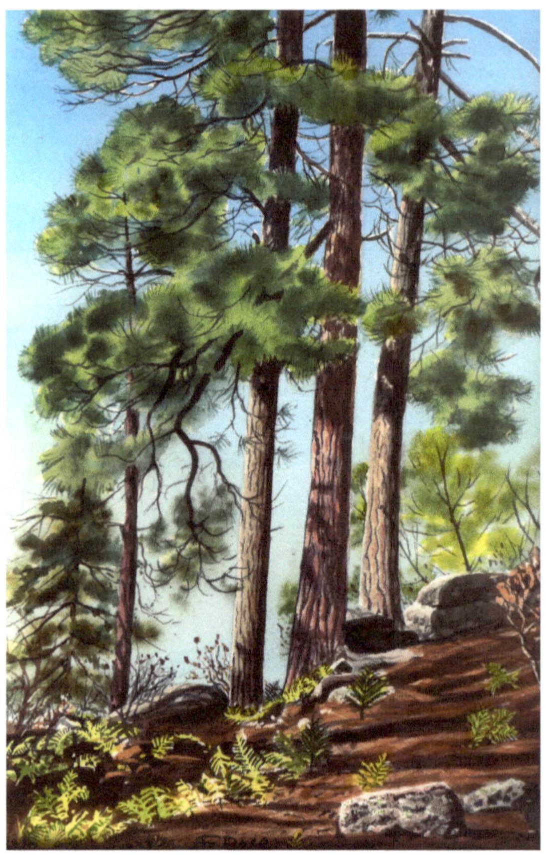

19. SUNSET TRAIL

There is a parking lot for the Sunset Trail across the road from the parking lot for the Butterfly trail. Two camp roads branch off at the end of the parking lot. North Sykes Nob Road veers to the right and the Soldier's Camp road goes more or less straight ahead. It is paved for a few yards, and then befomes a dirt road with cabins.

This dirt road has a kind of loop at the end, and along one side of the loop you can find the actual Sunset Trail. It is only 1.3 miles from this point to Marshall Gulch, with some very nice views of the Sabino Creek valley on the way. The painting shows a point along the trail where the view to the South begins to open up. Off a short distance to the left is a rocky outcrop where you can sit and enjoy a wonderful view of the valley. After this point the trail drops down, sometimes steeply, ending up in Marshall Gulch.

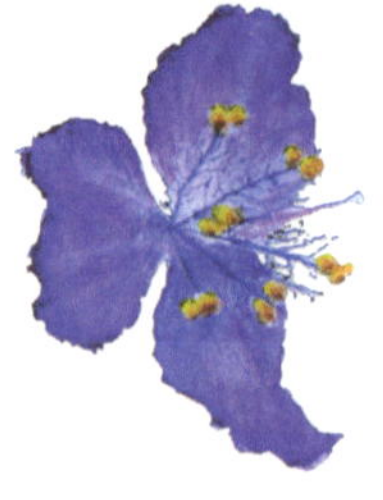

Spiderwort
Tradescantia pinetorum

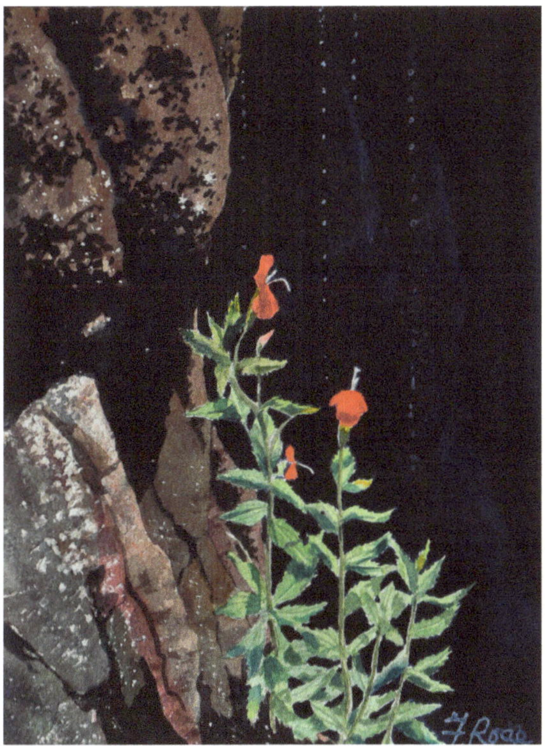

One of the first settlements in the mountain was called Soldier's Camp. Evidently it was used by the soldiers stationed at Fort Lowell, in Tucson. Civilian families built cabins there, near a stream that runs through this area. They did this long before the highway was built. All supplies had to be carried up on mules or horses.

Near the point where the Sunset Trail veers off to the right, there is a fork in the camp road. On the left it rises up to complete the loop connecting it to the part that leads back to the parking lot.

If, instead, you follow the road down hill, you come to an area where they had built a dam that created a lake. This was much loved by the inhabitants, but it eventually silted up. It was called Soldier Lake Tank. The dam is still there, and it still oozes water, as in this painting of Red Monkey flowers at its base.

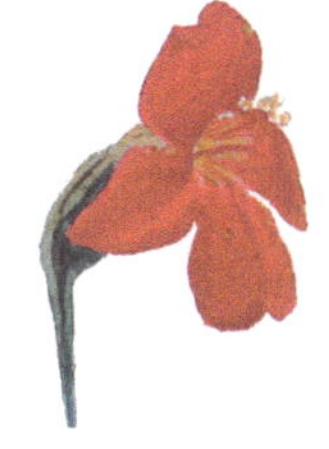

Red Monkeyflower
Erythranthe cardinalis

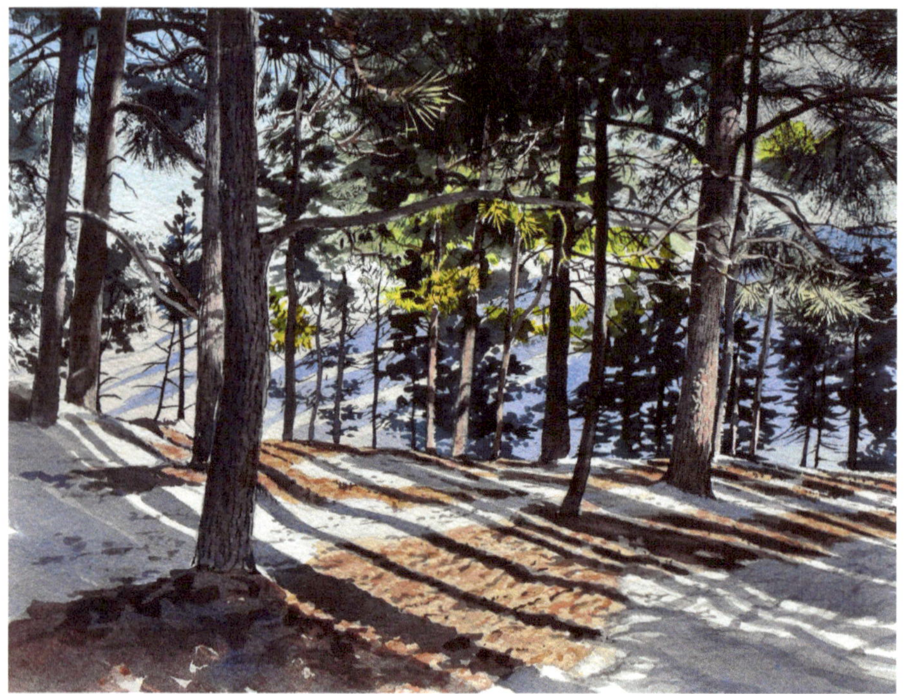

20. LOMA LINDA

After passing the Butterfly and then the Sunset Trail heads, the highway rises eventually levelling off. Inspiration Rock picnic area is on the left, and some distance past that there is a picnic area on the right. This is just before the road begins to slope down toward Summerhaven. This location is called Loma Linda (Spanish for Beautiful Hill). From it you can see the land north of the Catalinas. Looking to the right you can see Mount Bigelow with its many towers.

I was struck by the harmony of blue shadows in the distance going diagonally down to the left and shadows from the trees going to the right. When I took this picture several families were gathered around barbecues, and though there was snow on the ground they were dressed as if for the beach.

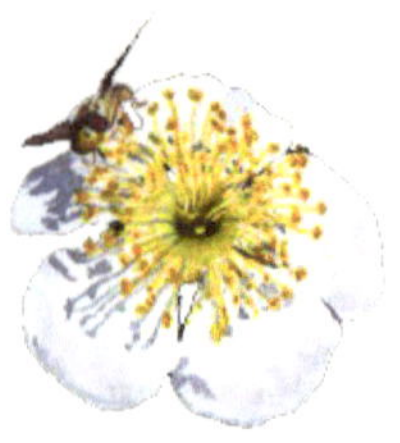

Cliff Rose
Purshia stansburiana

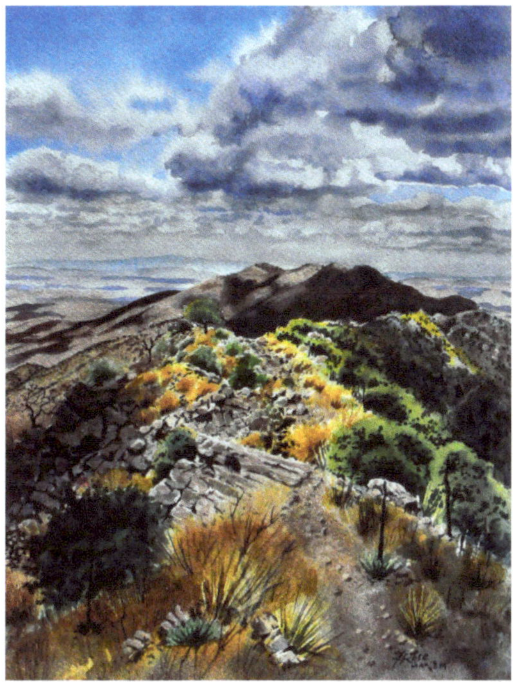

21. ORACLE RIDGE

Here is a view of Oracle Ridge, one of my favorite trails on the mountain. Long ago a road was built acessing the mountain range from the North. It is called the Control Road, because in those early days traffic times had to be controlled in a seven-mile stretch of the road where it was too narrow for cars to pass. There were set times for vehicles to drive up the road, and other times to drive down. It is about 25 miles long and tops out at the Mount Lemmon Fire Station. After turning right onto the Control Road, you pass the fire station on your right, and then drop down to a wide area just before the cattle grid. You can park here. The Oracle Ridge trail, which is part of the Arizona Trail system, goes off to the left, and the road goes straight ahead. Both of them go to Oracle, the trail being much shorter than the road since it goes in an almost straight line along a ridge. This part of the range is a favorite for wildflower lovers. After the summer rains the blooms are abundant and it is sometimes difficult to get through the masses of plants.

In the far distance you can just make out the area where one of Arizona's great beauty spots may be reached: Aravaipa Canyon, with its permanent stream.

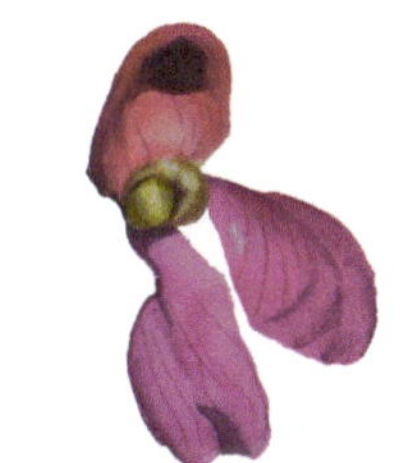

Gray's Lima Bean
Phaseolus grayanus

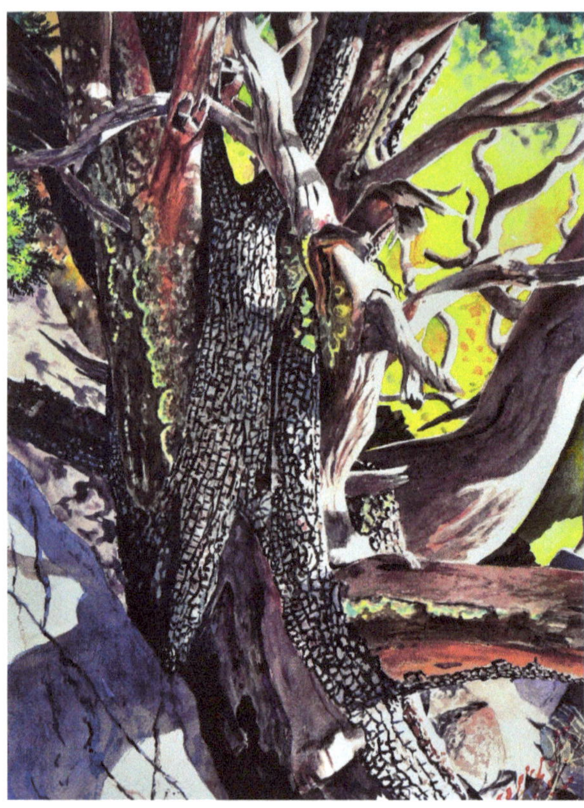

About a mile from the Oracle Ridge Trail head you come to a ridge, with views on both sides of the trail. Years ago I spotted this beautiful Alligator Juniper, demonstrating how it can survive with much of its bark missing. This tree species can be found from the Sabino Canyon, at the bottom of the mountain, to Oracle Ridge and even higher.

In two and a half miles you come to Dan Saddle. Before the two great fires of 2002 and 2003, there was a magnificent stand of these trees. These were victims of those fires. It was really sad to see these giants of the mountain cut down.

Parry's agave, like the Century Plant, lives year after year without blooming. When it is mature, it sends up a thick stalk, fifteen feet or more into the air, with lots of golden flowers at the top. One year hiking Oracle Ridge I saw many of the plants with stalks, but not yet in flower. I went back a week later to see the blooms. All the exposed stalks had all been broken off by the wind. Eventually I found a plant in a sheltered area with a stalk and clusters of gorgeous flowers.

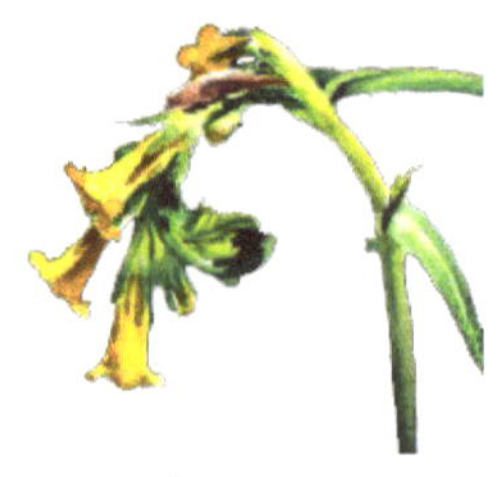

Purple Gromwell
Lithospermum multiflorum

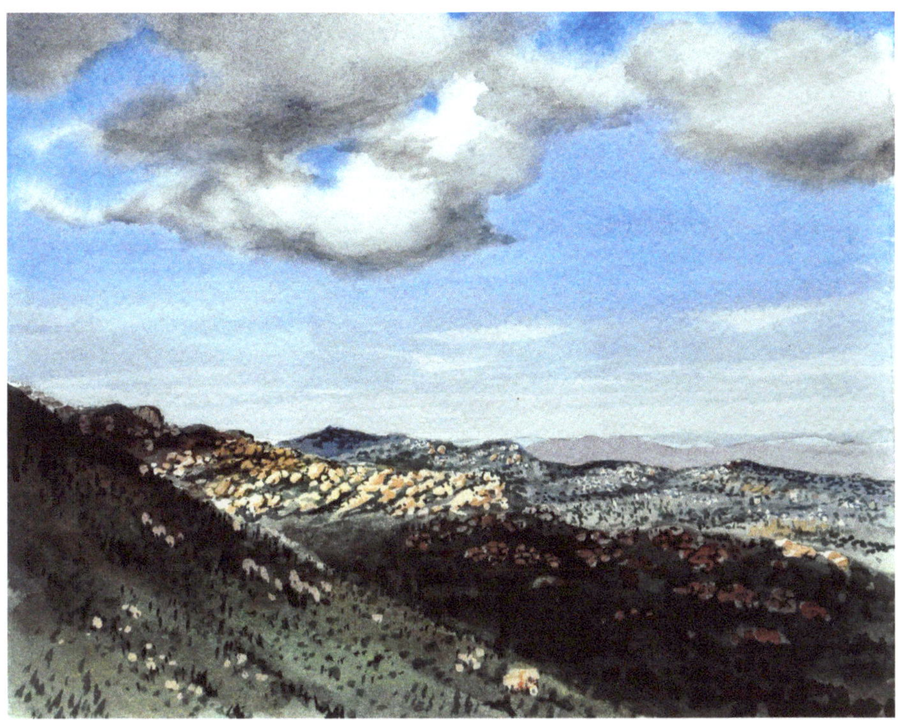

Looking to the left as you go along the Oracle Ridge trail, you can see this outcropping, called the Reef of Rocks. Beyond it is Oro Valley. The hills to the right in this painting block our view of Biosphere II.

Red Ridge Trail follows the ridge in the foreground of this painting. It drops down steeply to an old mining camp. From there you can take a trail to the right that rises to connect you with the Oracle Ridge trail at Dan Saddle, which is two and a half miles from its junction with the Control Road.

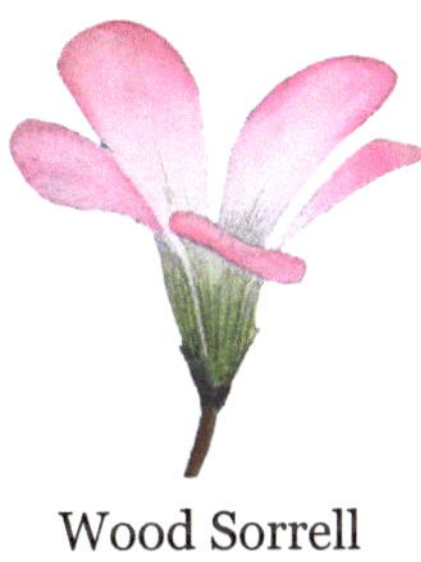

Wood Sorrell
Oxalis alpina

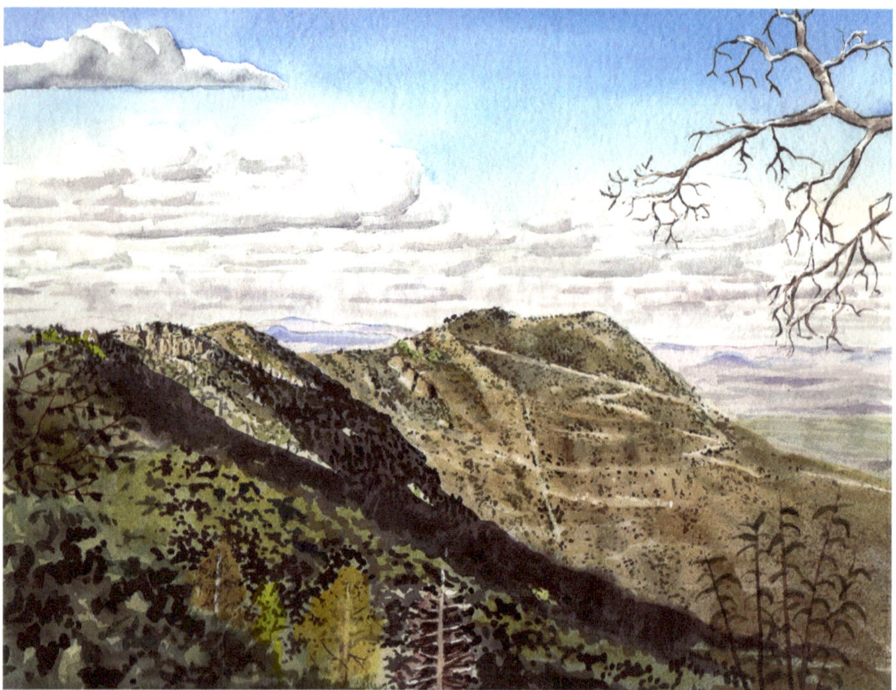

There are many signs of mining in the mountains, though most of them are hard to see. The zig-zag lines on this painting indicate an old mine road up Marble Peak. Once when we hiked to the top of the peak we found a jar with a list of *peak-baggers*, and I recognized one of the names, Bob Walko, as being the person who introduced us to the joys of hiking soon after we arrived in Tucson in 1982.

The mine is on the far side of this peak and has been reactivated. The trail follows the ridge on the left side of the picture.

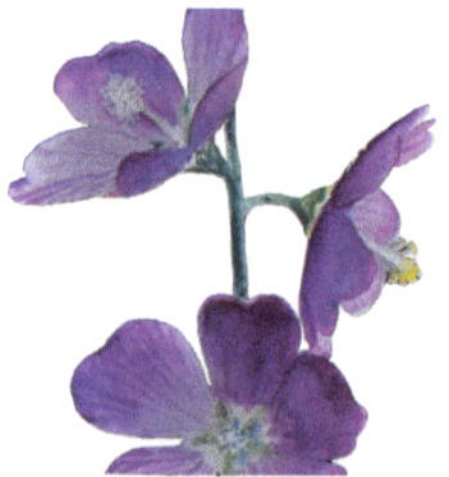

Fendler Globemallow
Sphaeralcea fendleri

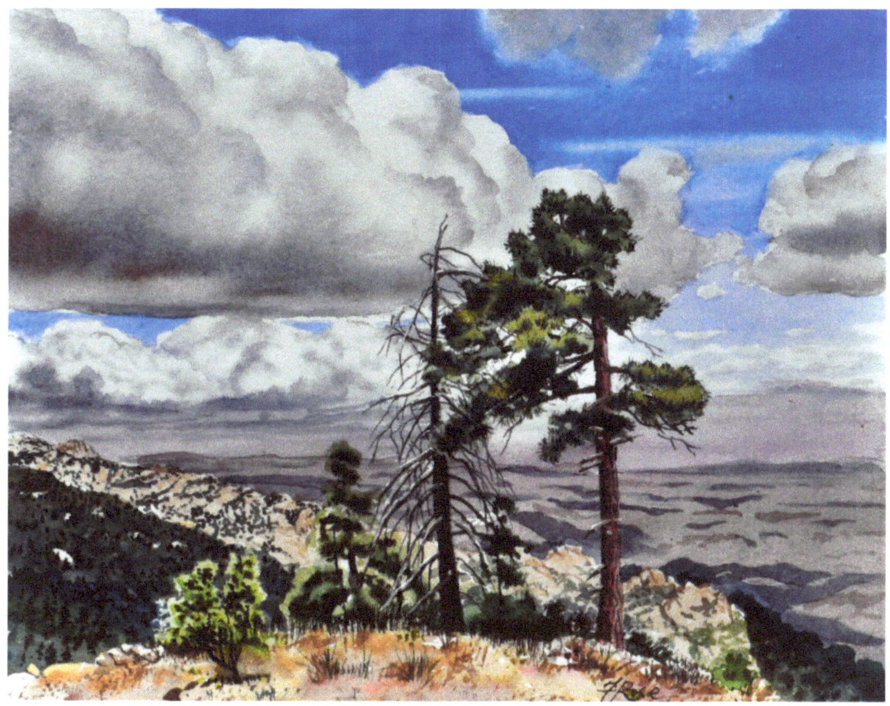

22. RED RIDGE

About half way up the road toward Ski Valley, there is a trail on the right called the Red Ridge Trail. It rises for a short distance, crossing a saddle area, and then drops sharply down the north side of the mountain.

After going through a densely wooded area, the trail comes to the opening shown in this painting, with a view of the Reef of Rocks and Samienego Ridge on the left, and Oracle Ridge on the right. Remains of an old mining camp are in the low spot directly below. Once there you can pick up a trail that heads to the right, rising to meet the Oracle Ridge Trail.

My wife, daughter and I hiked this loop to celebrate my sixtieth birthday. We found the climb back up pretty challenging, but the views were great.

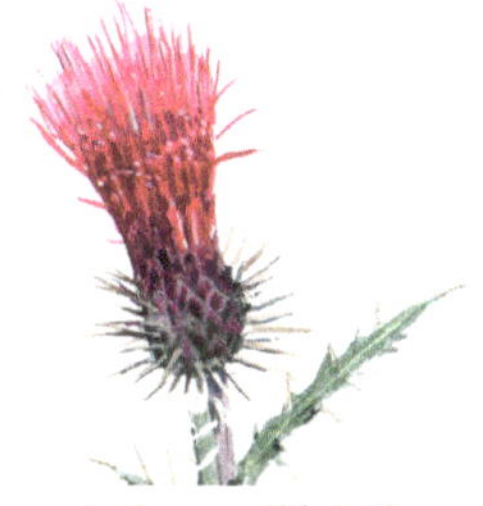

Arizona Thistle
Cirsium arizonicum

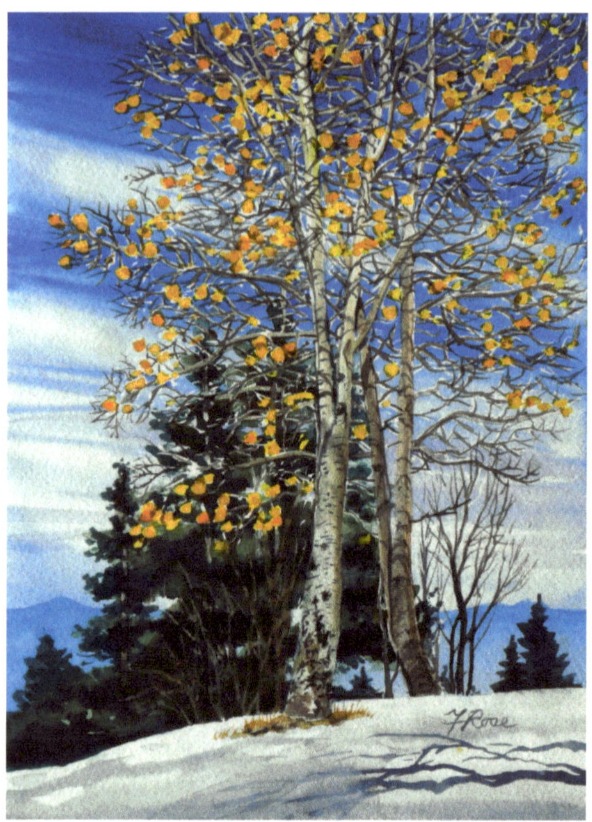

23. SKI AREA

As you drop down toward Summerhaven, there is a road off to the right that takes you to Ski Valley which has two parking lots. The parking lot on your right is always open. The painting shows an aspen on the slope leading up from that lot to the Iron Door Restaurant. Its indoor dining room has an enormous fireplace for cold wintry days. It was originally built as a Ski Lodge in the 1950's.

There is also dining on the porch, with multiple humming bird feeders, and a view of the ski slope. The parking lot on the left is for the ski slope and is locked at night.

This is the southernmost ski area in the United States. Some years there is plenty of snow, whereas in others there is not enough to ski, but the lift is open for people to enjoy the view. The road continues past this area to the top of the mountain.

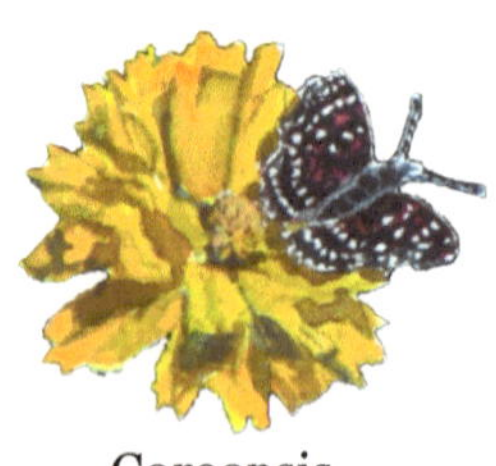

Coreopsis
Coreopsis sp.

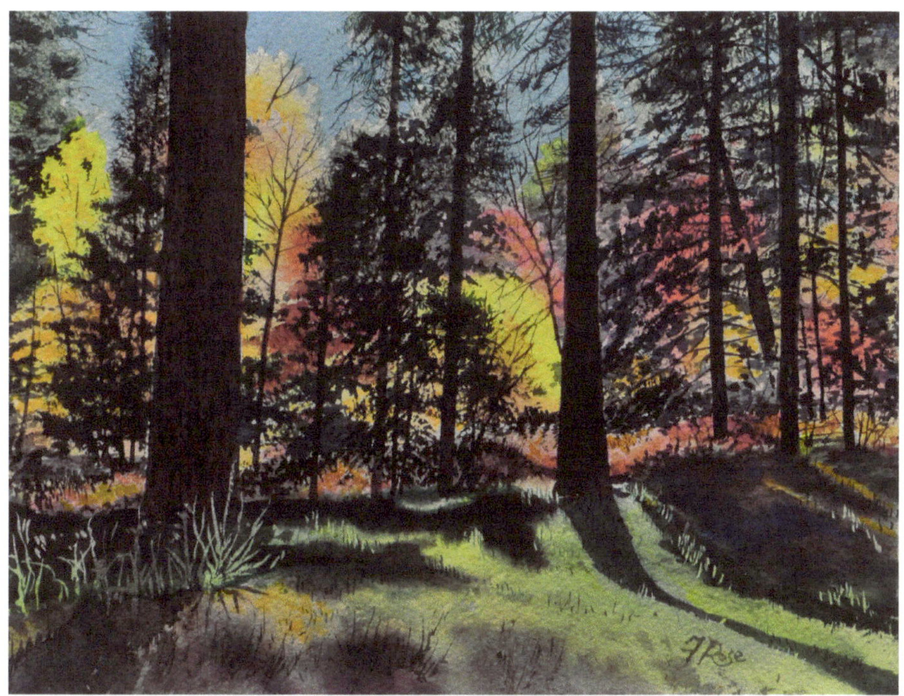

24. ASPEN DRAW TRAIL

From the parking lot below the Iron Door restaurant, you can see the ski slopes ahead of you, and a guard rail across the road on your left. Just over that rail is a trail that drops down to Turkey Run and then climbs a little over a mile and a half to the top of the ski run. This is a wonderful place to see fall colors.

Parts of the trail go through a thickly wooded forest. At one point the trail comes to the edge of one of the ski runs, then goes back into the forest emerging at the top of the mountain at just under 9000 feet.

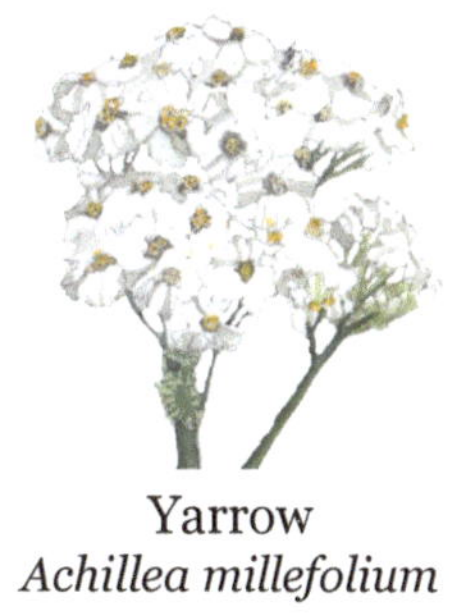

Yarrow
Achillea millefolium

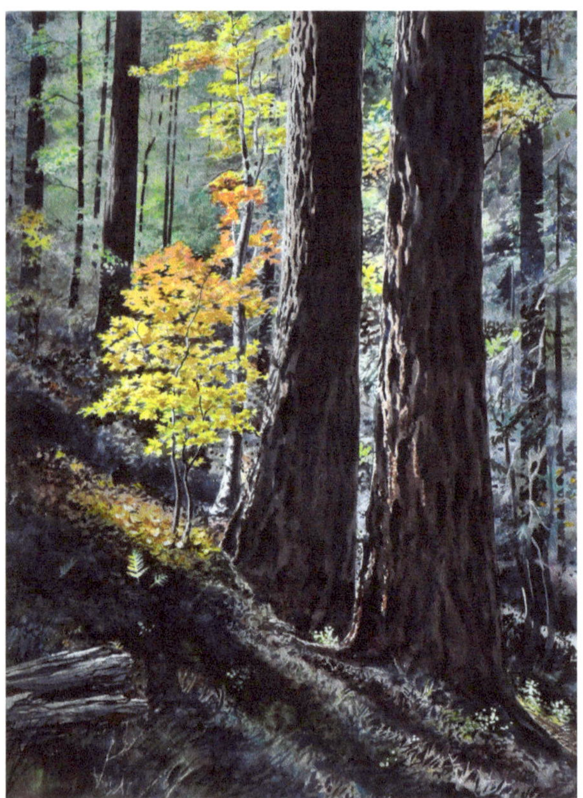

Since this is a north-facing slope of the mountain, it supports the growth of huge conifers. Here we see two Douglas Fir trees, with a Big Tooth Maple in its autumn gold, to the left. To the right of this picture you could catch glimpses of the ski slope, so beautifully green in the summer, and dazzlingly white in the winter. Here we are in between those two seasons. The sun is not as high in the sky as it was in full Summer, and many of the leaves on the deciduous trees have fallen, creating a carpet of soft color, and opening up the view into the woods.

The Aspen Draw Trail, or, as it is now called, the Aspen Trail is behind me in this picture. After hiking a short distance up the trail I know I will soon be in the middle of an aspen grove, with millions of golden leaves dancing in the sun.

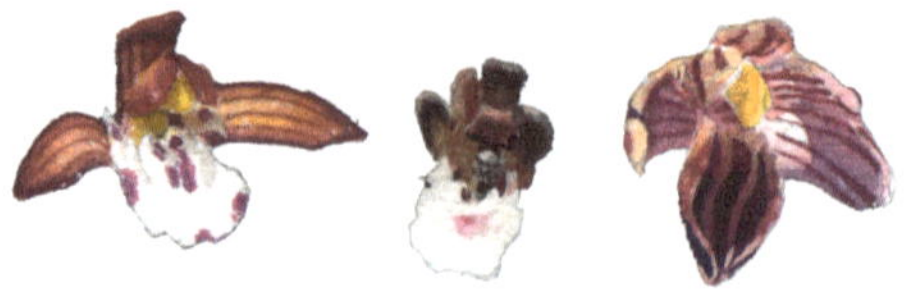

Spotted, Spring and Striped Coralroots
Corallorhiza maculata, wisteriana and striata

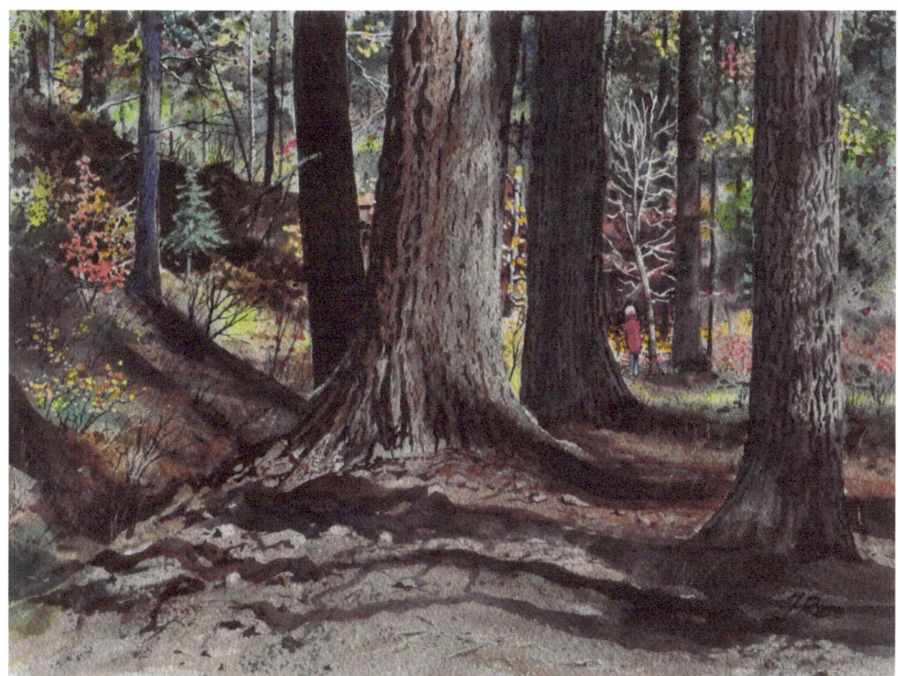

Continuing up the Aspen Trail, you enter an area of huge conifers, with a few maple trees scattered here and there. When I come into this area I think of Robert Frost's poem, with the line, "The woods are lovely, dark and deep."

My wife in red is disappearing up the trail. It is time for me to stop taking pictures and catch up with her. There are markers along this trail, though it is not clear now what they were marking.

This is a good place for walking among the Aspens, especially in October.

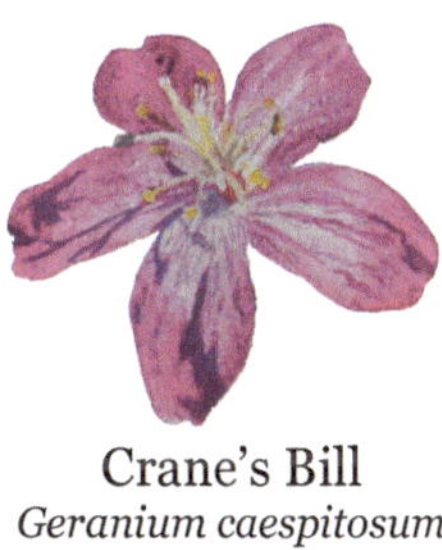

Crane's Bill
Geranium caespitosum

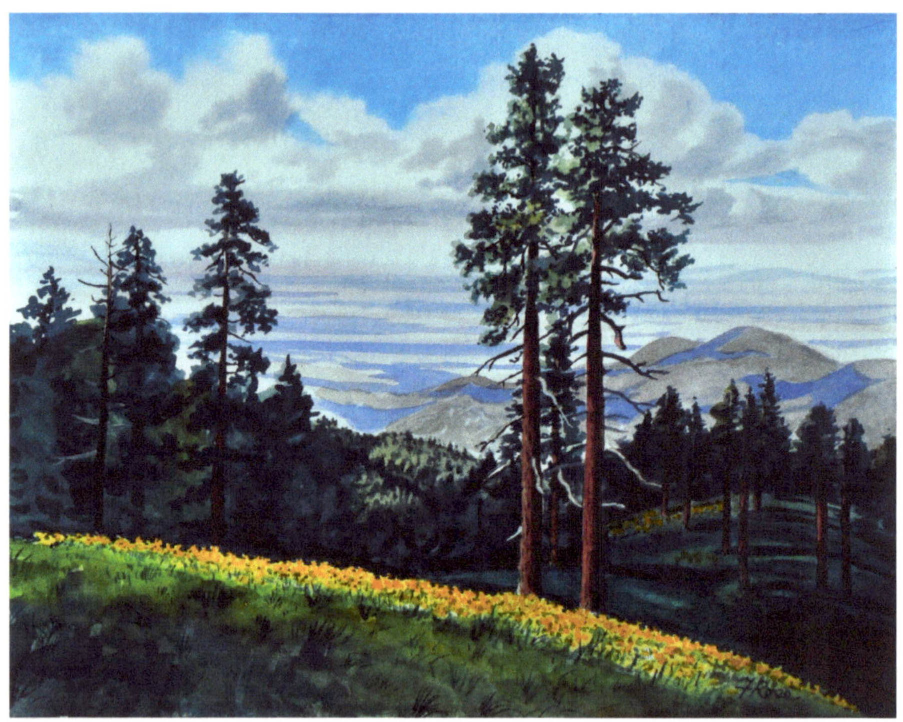

25. TOP OF THE SKI LIFT

At the top of trail, or the ski lift, you get this wonderful view to the north, with Oracle Ridge on the right, and beyond it Aravaipa Canyon. With powerful binoculars you might even be able to see the mines at Winkelman.

Straight ahead in the far distance is Pinal Peak south of Globe and past Globe, you come to Theodore Roosevelt Lake.

The flowers in this picture are Western Sneezeweed.

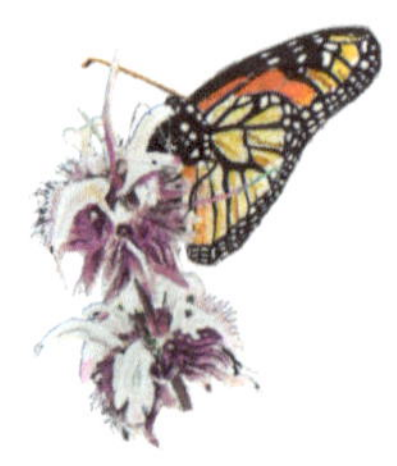

Beebalm
Monarda citriodora

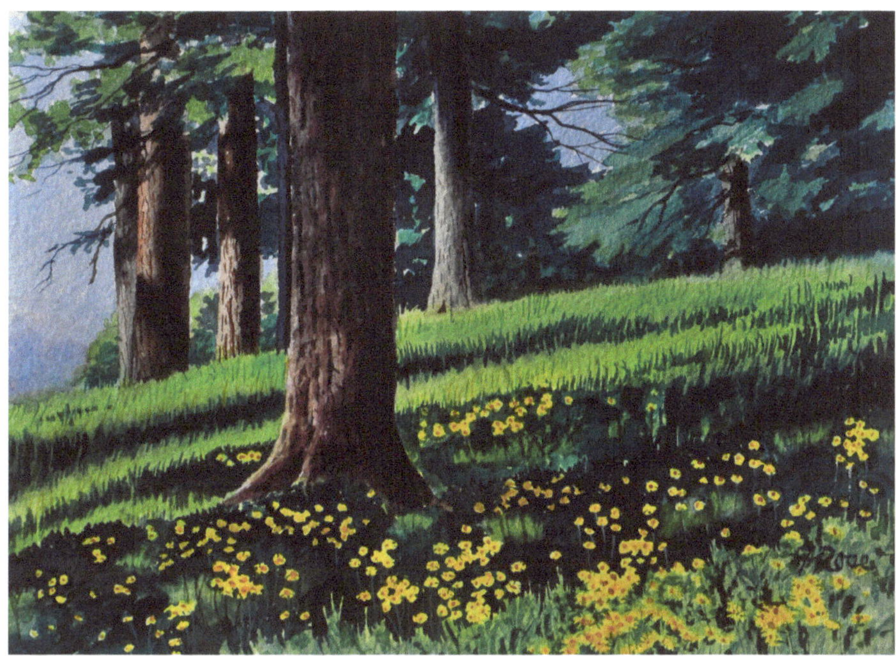

This is a view from the ski lift, just before it drops very sharply down. In the summer these beautiful trees shelter many wildflowers, especially the Western Sneezeweed.

The last time I took a ride on the lift, I was impressed with the beauty of the view to the North, and the otherworldly feeling of floating above the snow, which happened to be the last of the season.

The Ski lift runs more or less all year round. Some years the snow layer is deep enough for skiing.

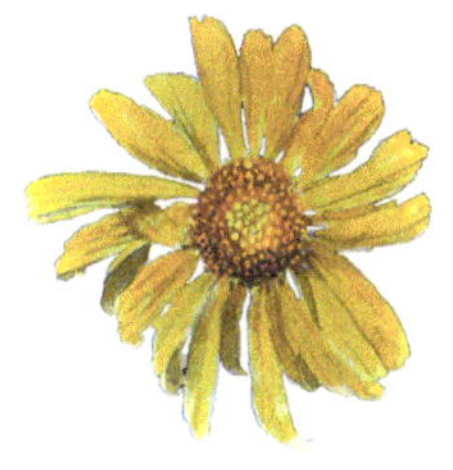

Western Sneezeweed
Hymenoxys hoopesii

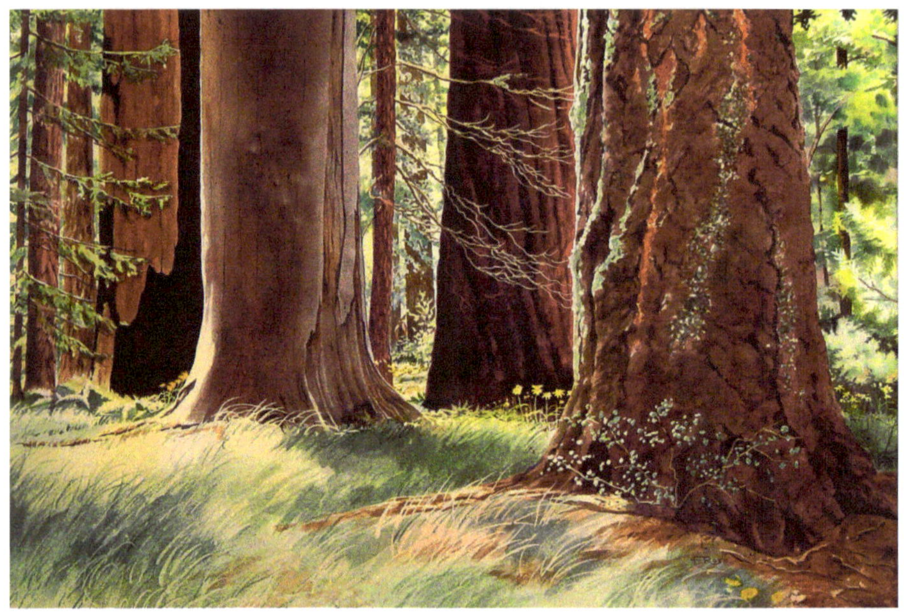

26. MEADOW TRAIL

Following the highway as high as it goes, you come to a gate leading to the Sky Center, with special observation nights. Turn left into a parking lot where you will find picnic tables and restrooms.

From the parking lot take the trail to the left of the transformer, with a trail map. Follow that a short distance up hill until you come to a dirt road. Go left on this road. Soon the Meadow Trail goes off to the right. It passes by the Sky Center,

Strictly speaking this is Mt. Lemmon, which is not a peak but is fairly flat. The path runs through a grassy area, then into some woods with huge Douglas fir trees standing like ancient Greek pillars and, after a short distance emerges into a beautiful meadow, a favorite picnic spot. Beyond the meadow the trail drops down the West side of the mountain.

Scouler's Catchfly
Silene scouleri

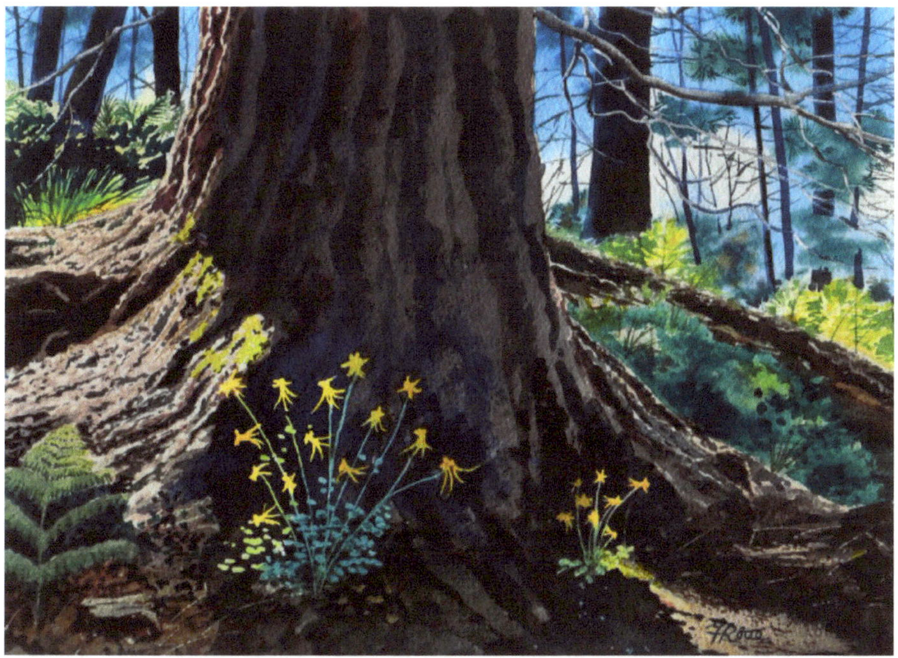

After leaving the meadow, the trail descends through an ancient forest.

One of my favorite stops on this part of the trail was beneath this very ancient Douglas fir, with columbines and other wildflowers at its base. The tree did not stand up straight but was leaning to the West and I marveled that it could hold itself up. It survived the fire, as it must have done during many fires in the past. Then, in the summer of 2015 it fell across the trail, revealing the fact that it had begun to rot near the base. I mourned the loss of this magnificent tree, one of the greatest giants of the forest.

The trail now skirts the remains of the fallen giant.

Golden Columbine
Aquilegia chrysantha

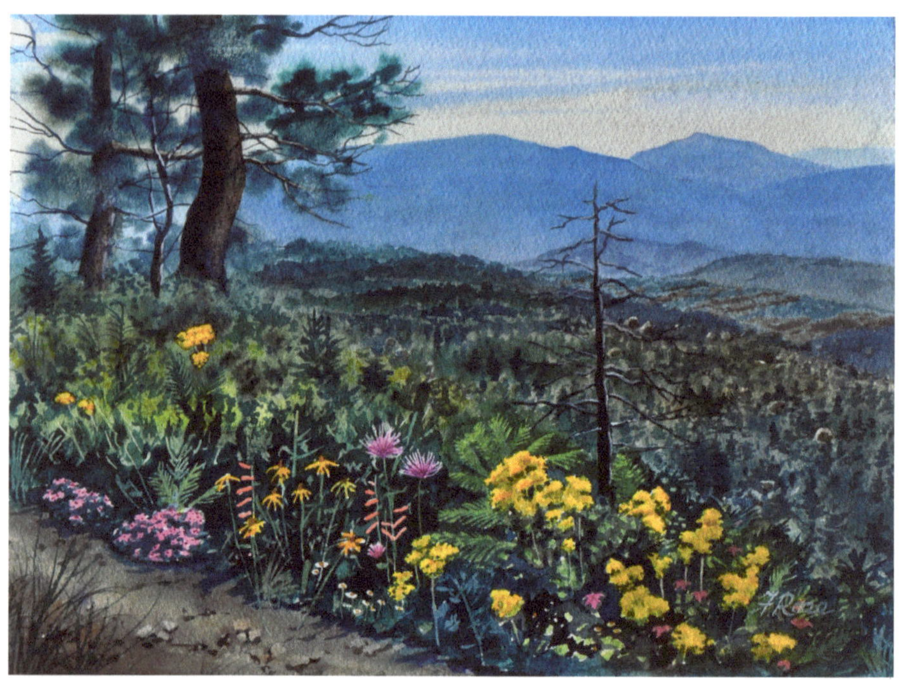

27. MOUNT LEMMON TRAIL

Back in the fifties, the Tricot electric company ran wires up the mountain and created a road to make access possible. This road drops down from near the top of Mount Lemmon.

After descending through the woods, you come to a place where a view of the valley opens up.

The Rincon mountains are in front of you, with Rincon Peak in the distance. After the summer rains the sides of this dirt road are deep in wildflowers.

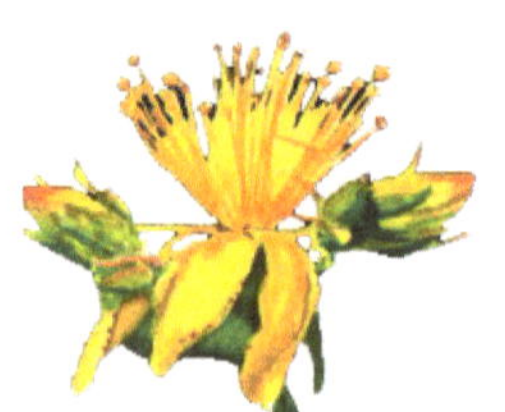

At one of the low points on the trail, there is a Spring, and many flowers surround the little shed housing it, including Saint John's Wort.

St. John's Wort
Hypericum formosum

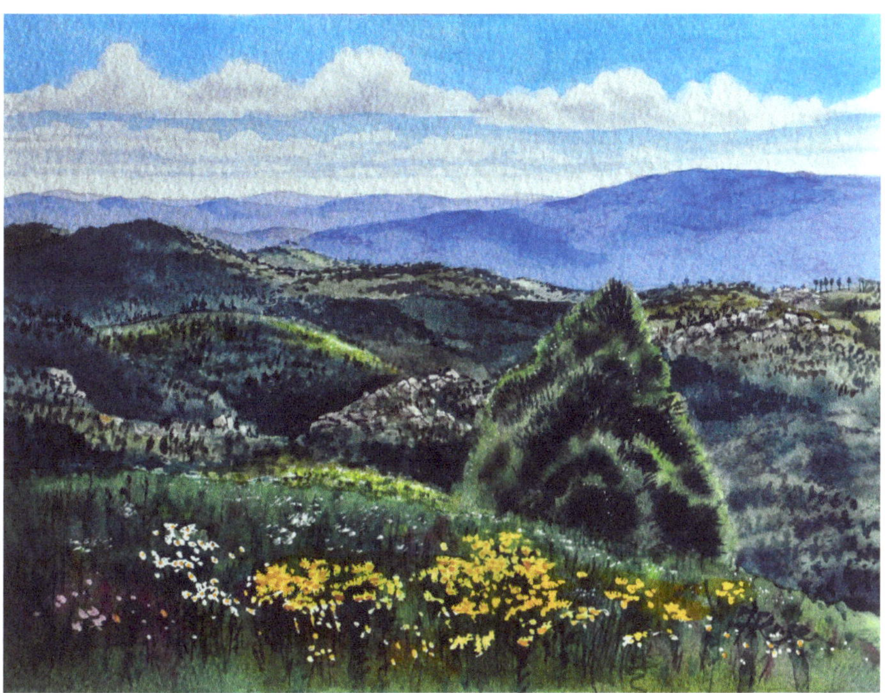

This is a slightly different view from the Mt. Lemmon Trail, with an abundance of wildflowers. There is a fairly long stretch along the road with these spectacular views to the North. Eventually the trail starts dropping down. The Meadow Trail connects with it on the right, and then it descends toward Catalina State Park.

There is an area in the valley directly below this ridge, called "The Wilderness of Rocks." This connects Marshall Saddle (to the East) with Romero Pass, (to the West) .

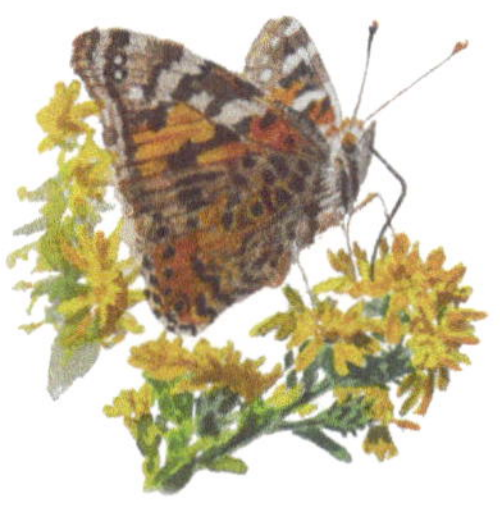

Sparse-Flowered Goldenrod
Solidago velutina

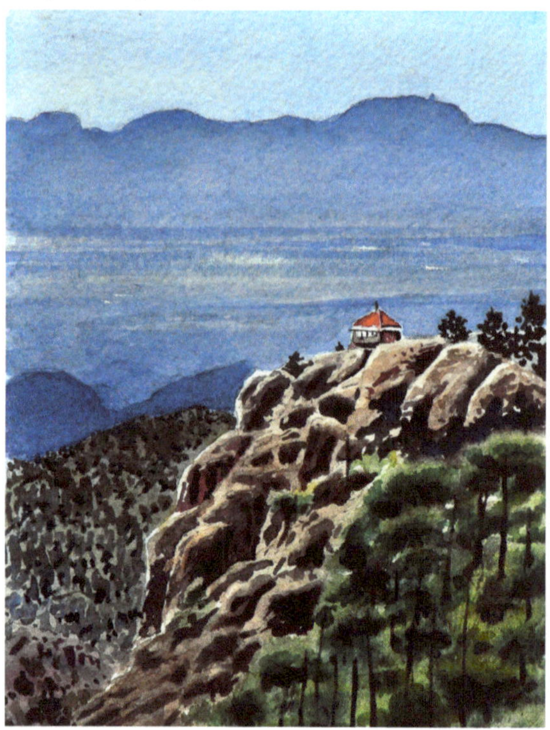

At the point where the Mountain Lemmon Trail opens up to
panoramic views of the valley, there is a side road going off to the
left. At the end of this road there is a large rock formation with steps
leading up to a fire lookout.

The lookout was built in 1928 and is used in the early summer
months. It sits at 8,720 feet. In the distance in this painting, you can
see the relatively flat area of Kitt Peak in the Quinlan mountains.
With binoculars you can make out some of the 22 optical and 2 radio
telescopes on that peak. You might also be able to see the McMath–
Pierce Solar Telescope with its long shaft sloping down on the left side
of the peak.

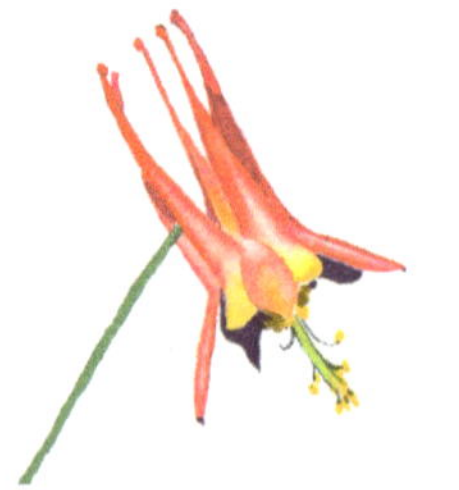

Most of the columbines on the mountain are
pure yellow, but there are some at the base of
this rock that are red and yellow.

Desert Columbine
Aquilegia desertorum

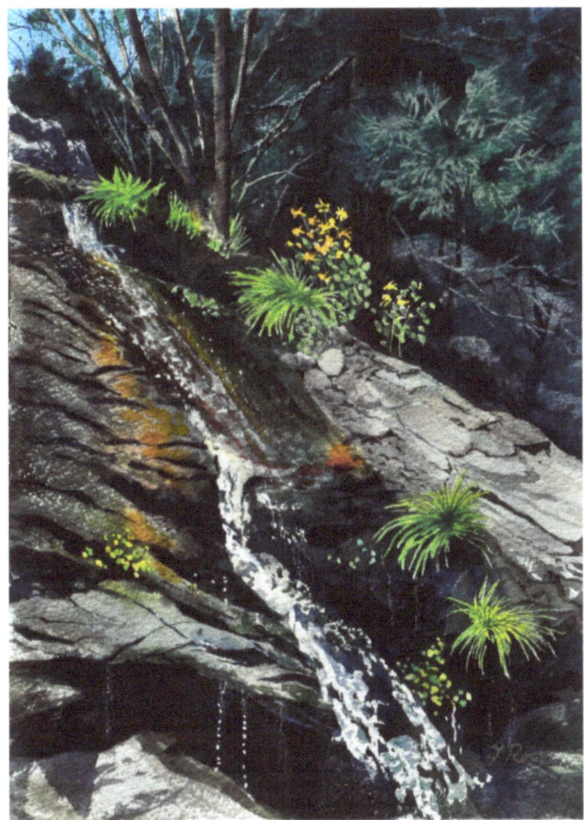

28. MARSHALL GULCH

Once you have driven through Summerhaven, and past the school house on the right, you come to a parking area with a gate (which is closed in the winter months). This painting shows an intermittent waterfall just past the gate, that is often rich with wild flowers, including Western Sneezeweed, and the Yellow Monkey Flower, depicted in the cameo below.

The main parking in the Gulch is about a half mile further down the road, with three trail heads: Marshall Gulch Trail, Aspen Trail (that does a loop connecting with that first trail), and the Sunset Trail. There is no sign indicating where the Sunset Trail begins. To reach it, go to the end of the parking lot, down into the stream and cross it. The trail takes you to an area with cabins, and a dirt road that ends up at the Hitchcock Highway between mile posts 22 and 23.

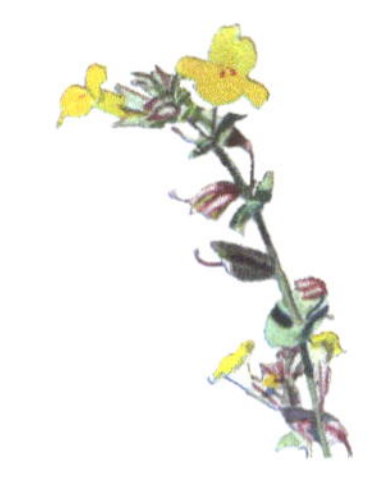

Yellow Monkeyflower
Erythranthe guttata

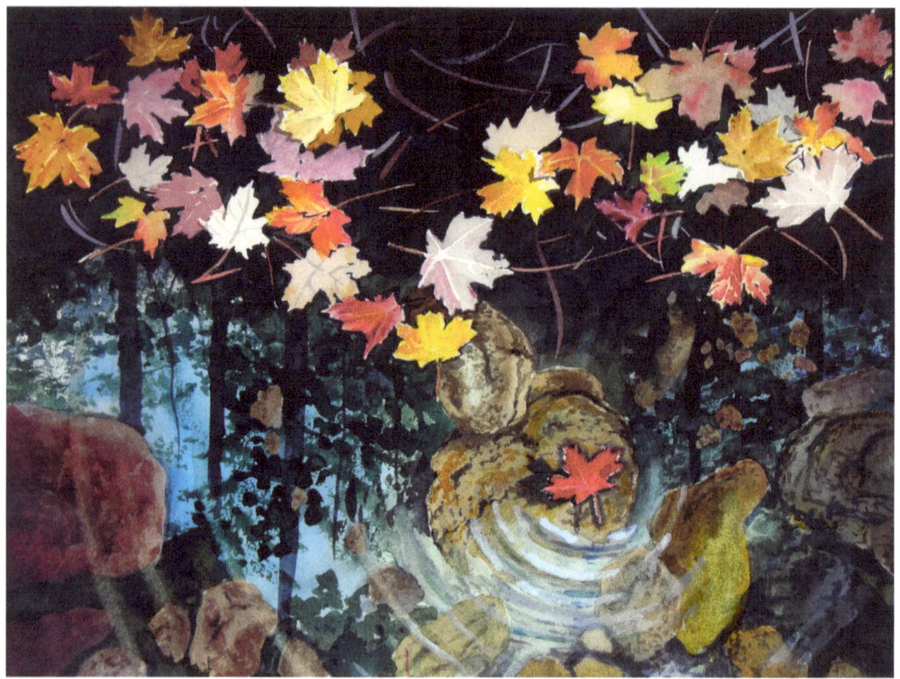

The Fall is a great time to enjoy Marshall Gulch. The air is clear and crisp after the Summer rains, and the shadows have started to lengthen.

Marshall Creek flows down from Marshall Saddle, to join Sabino Creek in the parking lot. There are many maple trees along the creek. The Rocky Mountain Maple trees have pale yellow leaves, but the Big Tooth Maples can have a range of colors from pale yellow to deep red. They have a special beauty when floating on the water with the blue sky reflected beneath them.

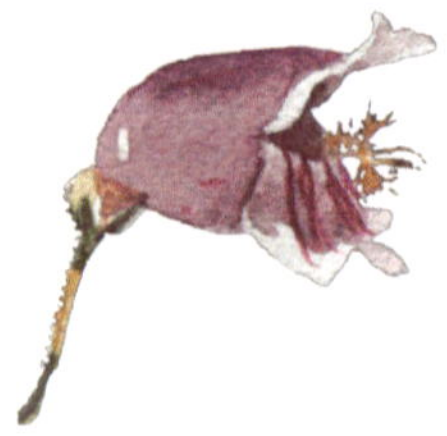

Palmer's Penstemon
Penstemon palmeri

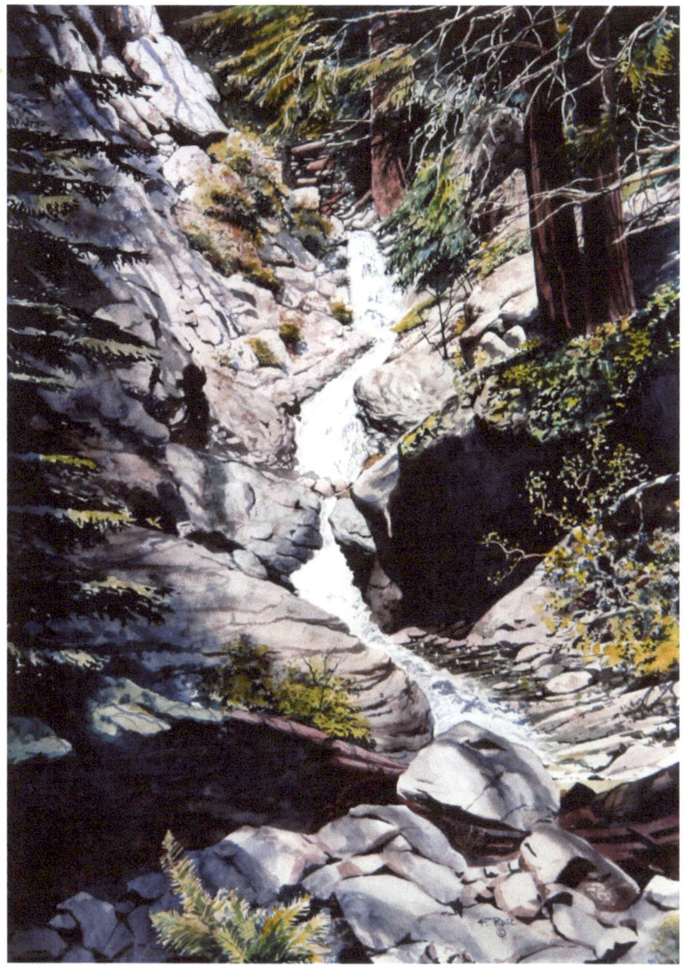

Sabino Creek runs through Marshall Gulch, descending through rocky areas on its way down to Sabino Canyon. This painting shows a portion of the creek some distance below the Marshall Gulch parking area.

The Sunset Trail goes near this area. It is possible, though difficult, to follow Sabino Creek some distance although the vegetation can be almost impassible.

There is at least some water in this part of the creek most of the year. Below this area it goes underground in the dry months, mostly in Spring and early Summer.

Longtube Ipomopsis
Ipomopsis tenuituba

Marshall Gulch 75

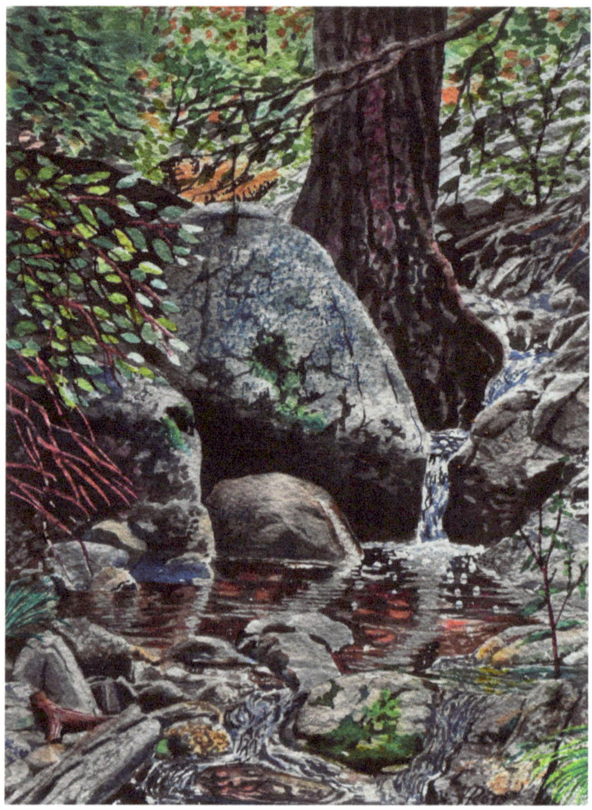

Long ago there was at least one cabin in Marshall Gulch. Water flows in the creek most of the year, with charming little waterfalls and occasional pools. Trying to capture the beauty of this area is quite a challenge for the artist.

The red branches in the left side of this painting belong to the Red Osier Dogwood, one of the most abundant shrubs in this part of the mountain range. It blooms in the Spring with clusters of beautiful white flowers, with pink accents.

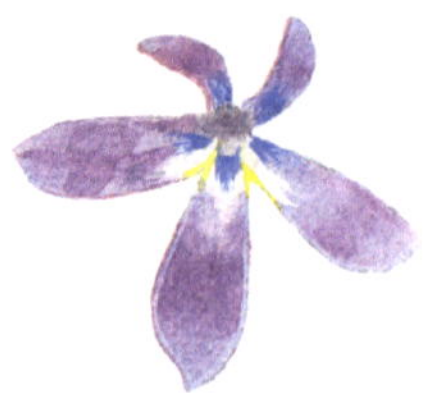

The pools attract all kinds of insect life and small children.

Apache Lobelia
Lobelia anatina

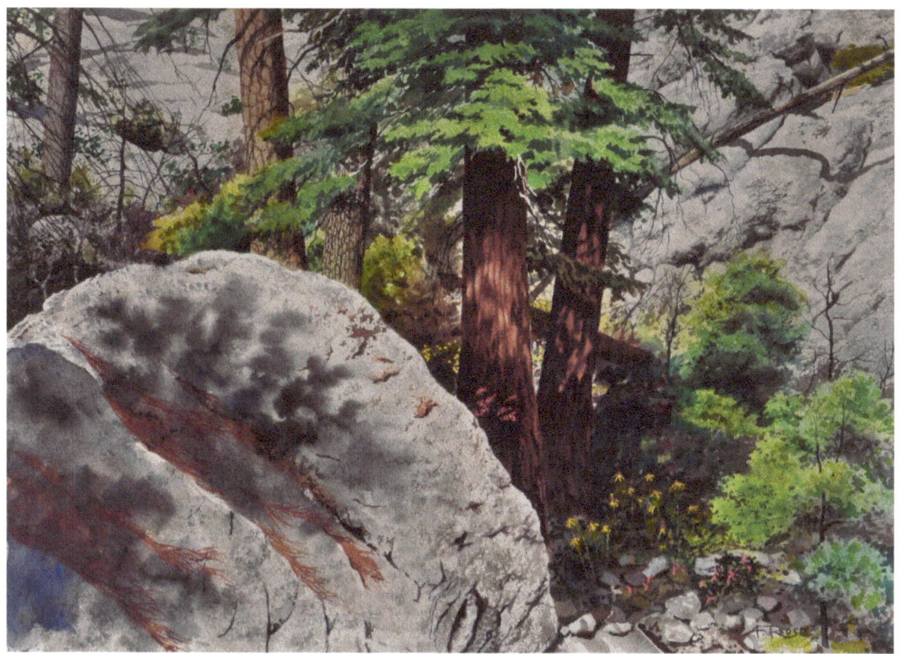

This is another view of the rocks below Marshall Gulch. Sabino Creek runs through this area. The Cutleaf Coneflower shown in the cameo, and in the painting, thrives in these moist stream beds, with plants up to four feet tall. Some huge boulders have tumbled into the gully, and many plants flourish there.

When I explore regions like this I look for rare and beautiful flowers, some of them quite small.

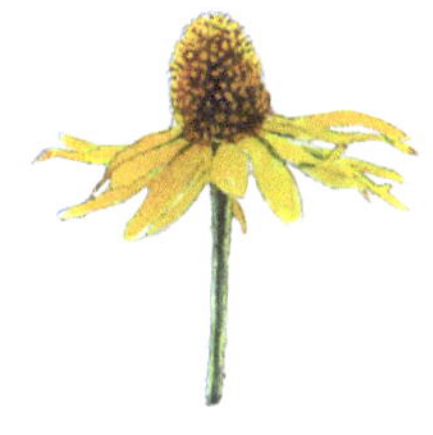

Cutleaf Coneflower
Rudbeckia laciniata

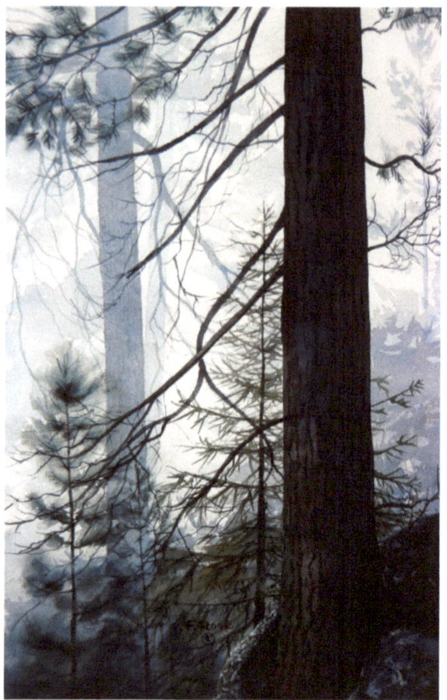

29. SUMMERHAVEN

Taking advantage of the Homestead Act of 1862, in about 1882 Frank Weber acquired 160 acres in what is now Summerhaven. In 1917 his land was bought by the Summerhaven Land and Improvement Company. The first cabin in this range was built in 1908, long before there was any road up from the valley. The little town of Summerhaven on the top of the mountain was founded in 1939, by Tony Zimmerman, whose hand, minus two fingers, is on the shirts of the staff in the Sawmill Run Restaurant in the center of town.

During a period of over 30 years my wife and I have rented cabins for a week or two, or even a month, in Summerhaven. We have been in at least eight various cabins. This painting was done of the view from the window of one of those cabins, a typical Summerhaven view, though less so now that more of the trees have been removed because of being too close to the cabins.

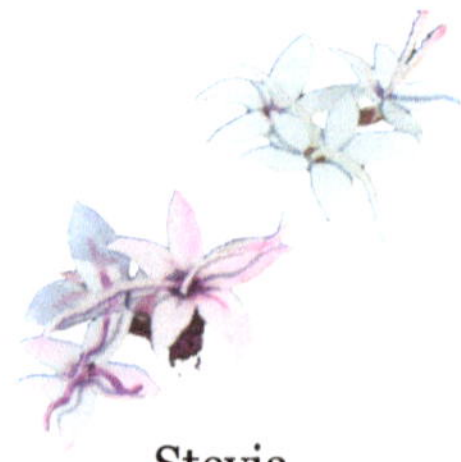

Stevia
Stevia serrata

There are two restaurants here - The Iron Door and Sawmill Run Restaurant, plus the Cookie Cabin which also sells pizza. There is also the Living Rainbow gift shop, the General Store, a Post Office and a Community Center. The fire station is at the top of the Control Road.
Some people live here year-round, and there is even a school for the children.

Chapter Four:
What to see on the way down

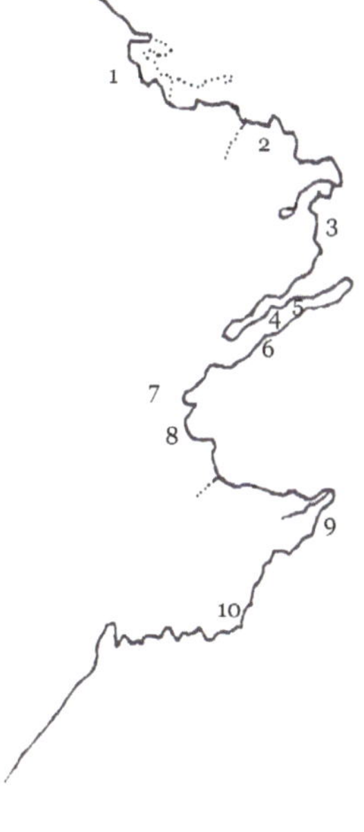

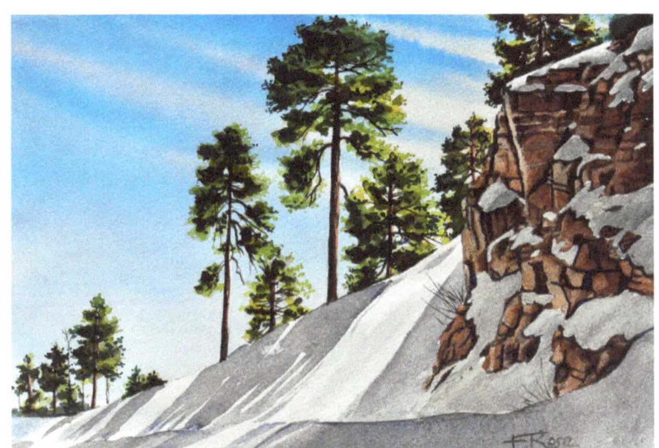

1. BY THE WHITETAIL CAMPGROUND

There are a number of views that you are likely to see on the return journey that you did not notice on the way up the mountain. For much of the trip, you are looking South. You might be able to see the Santa Rita mountains far in the distance, with the Tucson Mountains on your right, and the Rincon Mountains on your left. In between you and the Rincons is Aqua Caliente (Hot Springs) Hill.

You can see how the Catalinas and Rincons with Agua Caliente Hill in between, form one sky island. The only public road system is in the Catalinas. The other parts have various trails, but no paved roads.

It is possible that the sun is descending in the West on this ride home. Even if you have gone to the very top of the mountain, it will take you less than an hour to reach the bottom, and there are some spectacular views to add to your enjoyment of the final leg of your outing. My eye often enjoys seeing a very flat slab of rock slanting down. This is just before Whitetail Campground. It is especially dramatic when it is covered with snow.

Palmer's Lupine
Lupinus palmeri

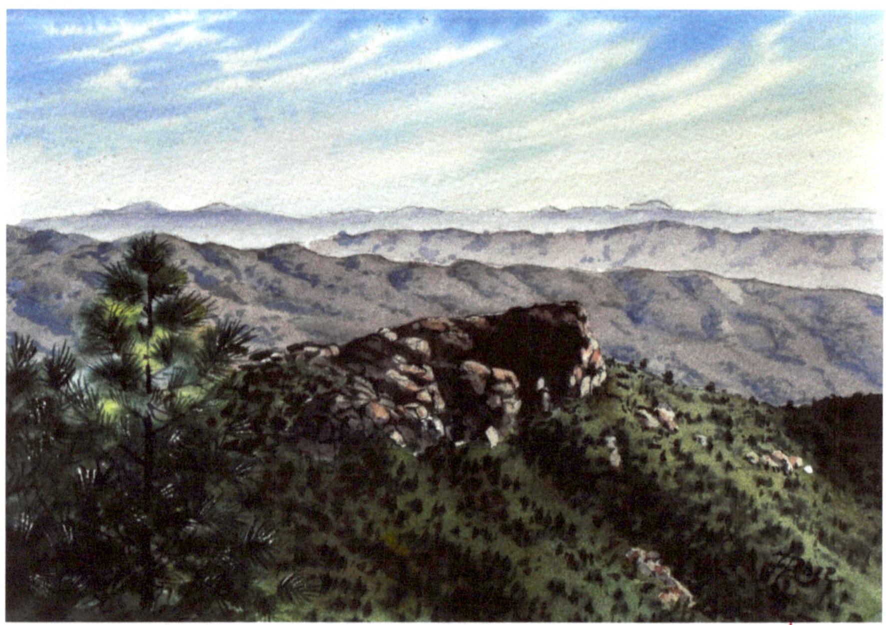

2. VIEW OF LIZARD ROCK

Soon after passing the Palisades Ranger Station, views start opening up on the right side of the road, and it is possible to get a glimpse of Lizard Rock. This granite outcrop has a high point on its Western end, giving the impression of the head of a lizard. It is possible to climb this rock, though there is no trail and the way is steep and covered with loose gravel. From the top you can see Willow Canyon, with its cabins, as well as Rose Canyon Lake to your right, and almost the whole of Tucson to the South.

There is pull off parking near the base of the rock.

Caltrop
Kallstroemia grandiflora

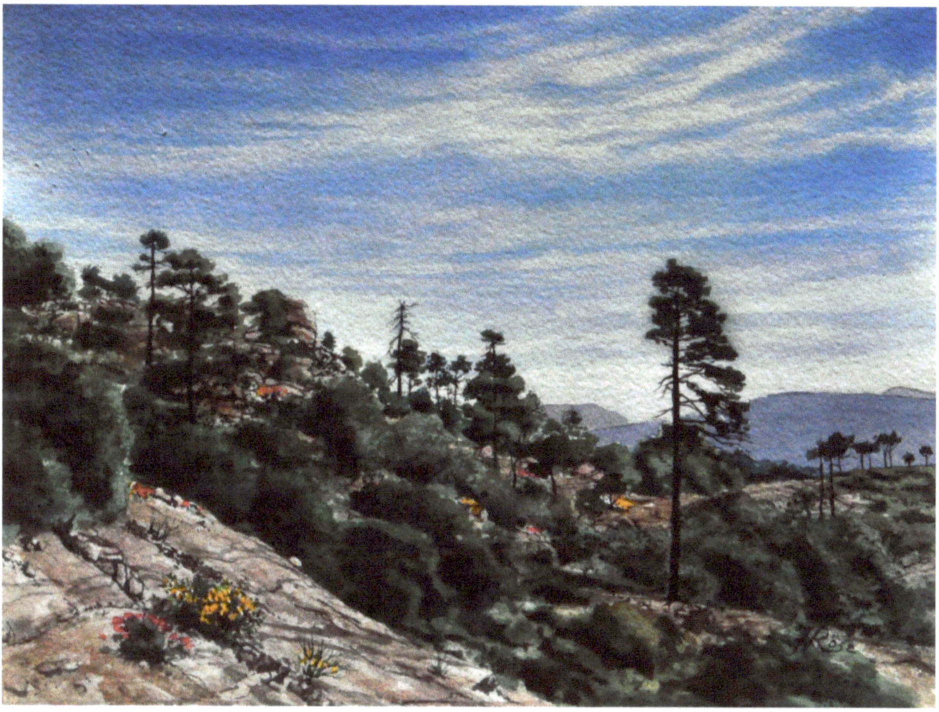

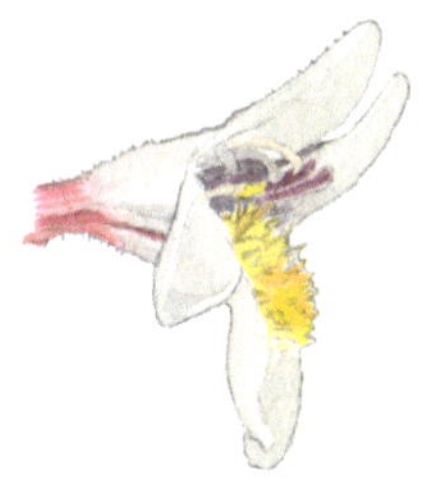

3. BY LIZARD ROCK

Lizard rock is to the right of this painting, with the Rincon mountains
in the distance. After passing this area, you come back into a view of the
Tucson valley.

The top of the slope on the left side of this painting is Green Mountain.
The Green Mountain Trail goes around the east side of this peak and then
drops into the Hithcock camp ground, a thousand feet below.

Catalina Beardtongue
Penstemon discolor

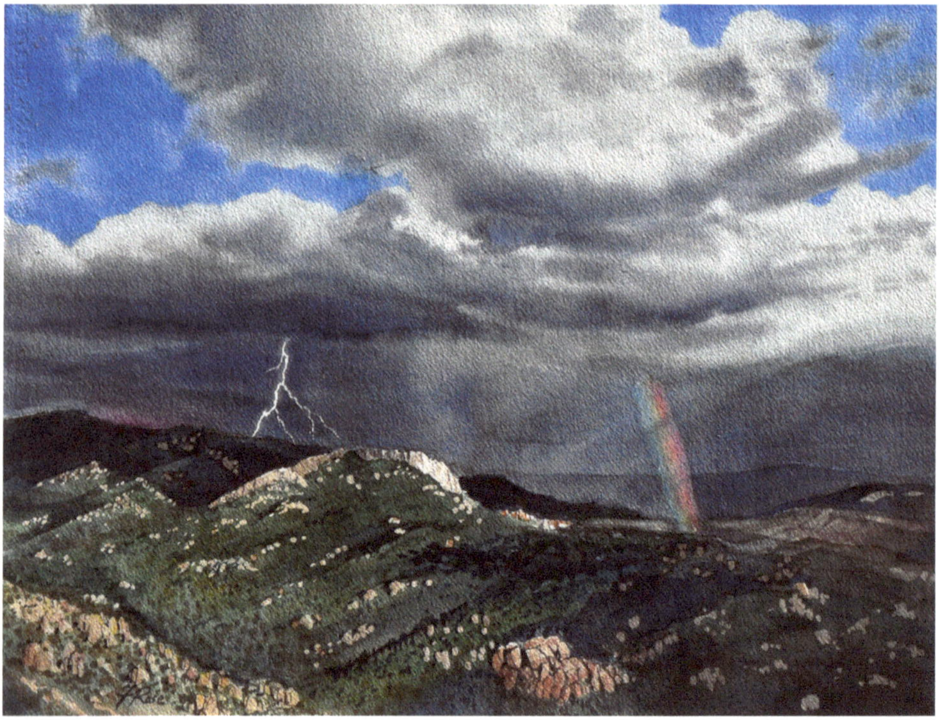

4. BELOW WINDY POINT

One day after passing Windy Point we caught a monsoon storm over Bear Canyon. In the far distance you can see the mountains near Wilcox.

The two-mile drive down the highway from Windy Point to Hitchcock campground, affords wonderful views to the right. The curve at the bottom of the slope takes you back into the pine forest, with Chihuahua Pine on the right side of the road, and Middle Bear and Cypress picnic areas on the left.

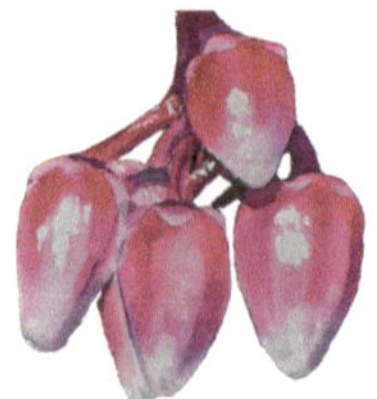

Manzanita
Arctostaphylos pungens

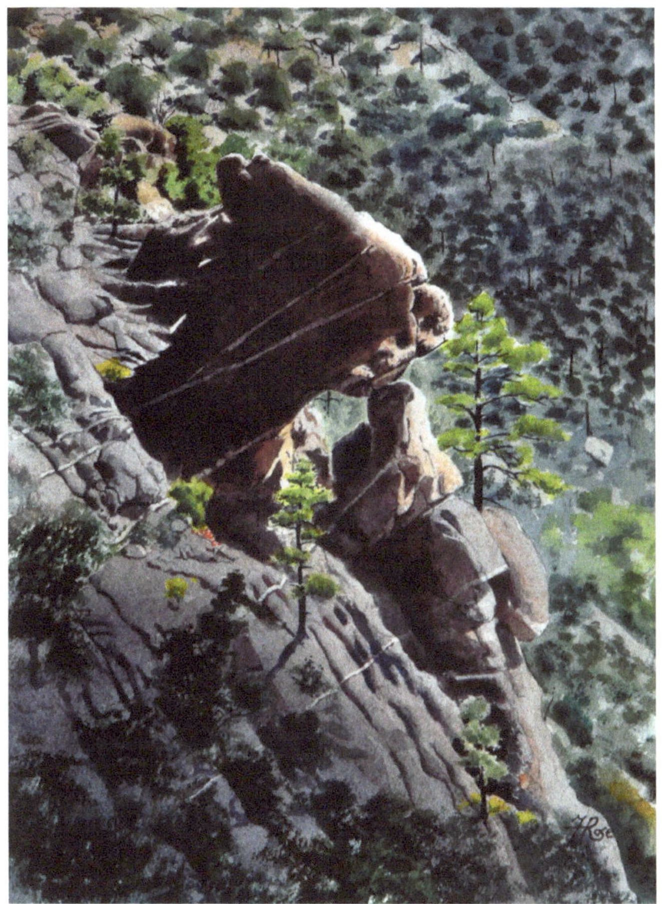

5. THE LITTLE WINDOW

Toward the bottom of the two mile slope after leaving Windy Point, and before you get to the Hitchcock campground, you might catch a glimpse of this rock formation on your right. It is shaped more or less like a shark's fin that is pierced with a little window. The trees in this part of the mountain are a mixture of Ponderosa Pine, Southwestern White Pine and, unique to this part of the mountain, the Chihuahuan Pine. This is largely a Mexican species, reaching its northern limit in this mountain range. After the hair-pin bend at the entrance to the Hitchcock campground, you will find a picnic area named after it on your right. This a very pleasant place to stop and enjoy the mountain air. It is also home to a number of wildflowers and birds. We particularly notice the Acorn Woodpeckers and Mexican Jays, eagerly awaiting scraps from your lunch.

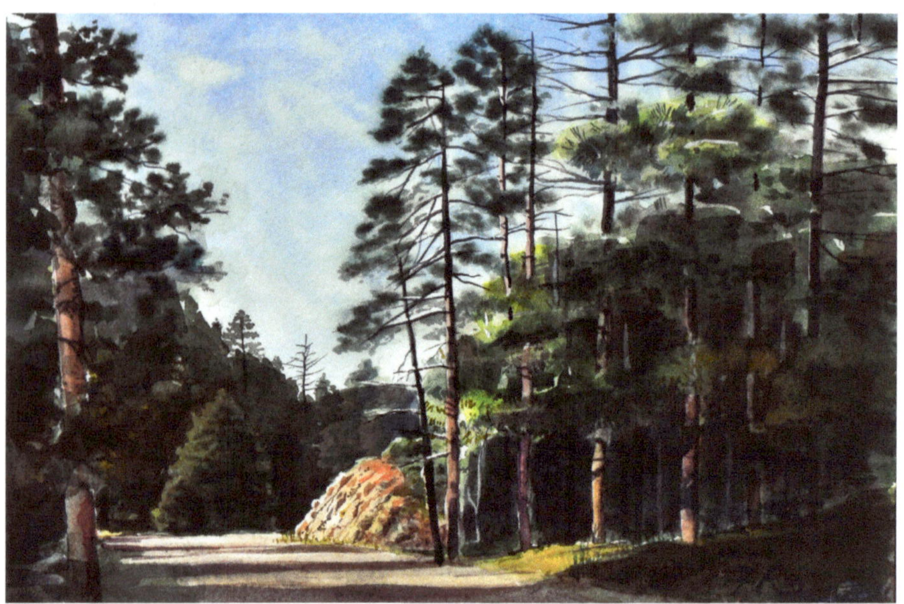

6. BEAR CANYON

Driving through Middle Bear, just before you pass the Cypress picnic area, you might catch the evening light highlighting some of the rocks and trees. The pine trees here are mostly Ponderosa with some Chihuahua Pine, a Mexican species that reaches its northernmost point in the Catalina mountains.

For the painting I omitted a sign in front of the rock that indicated that Cypress picnic area is on the left.

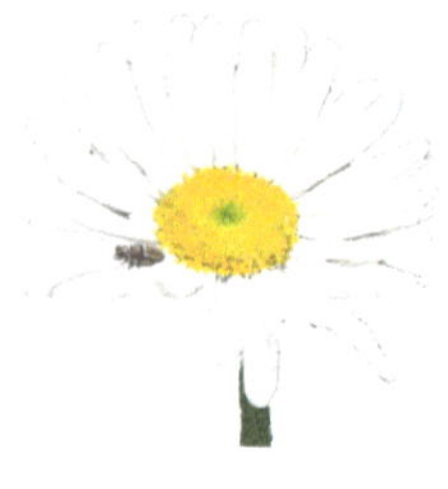

Fleabane
Erigeron divergens

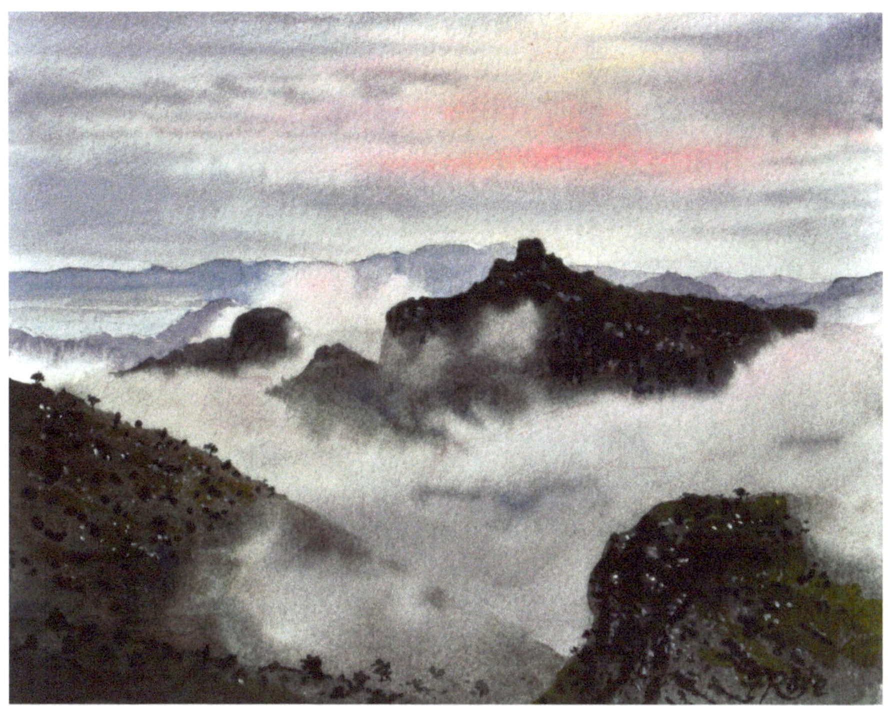

7. THIMBLE PEAK

If you pull off to the right to look at the Seven Cataracts, your eye might be drawn to the course of the creek as it descends to Seven Falls, with Tucson in the distance.

On this trip down we saw Thimble Peak rising above a cloud layer that filled Sabino Canyon, to the right, and Bear Canyon, to the left. Sycamore Reservoir, now entirely silted up, is covered with clouds at the bottom of this picture.

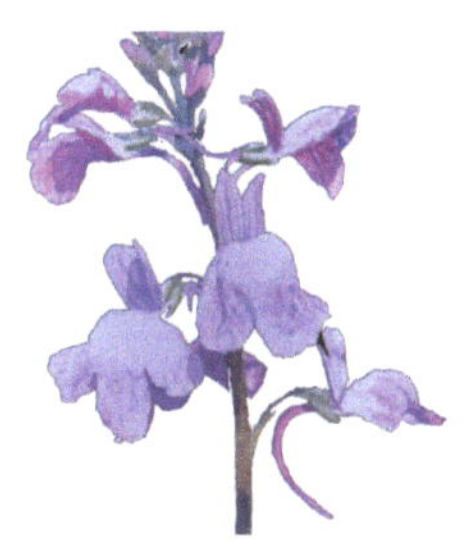

Texas Toadlfax
Nuttallanthus texanus

85

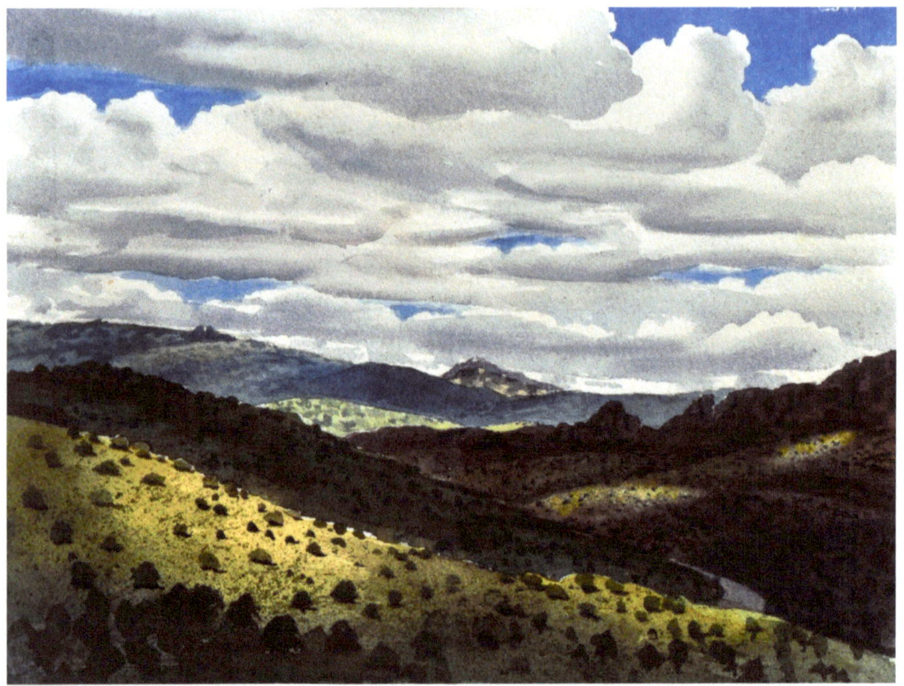

8. VIEW OF RINCON PEAK

This is the view at about mile post eight. Gordon Hirabayashi camp is in the lower right of the picture. When we first hiked this trail many years ago, there was a Saguaro on the Bug Spring trail, about in the lower center of this painting. It was growing at over 5000', the upper limit at which Saguaros can survive.

Rincon Peak is the most distant point in the views. Most of the dark green spots on the hillside are oak trees with lots of grass in between.

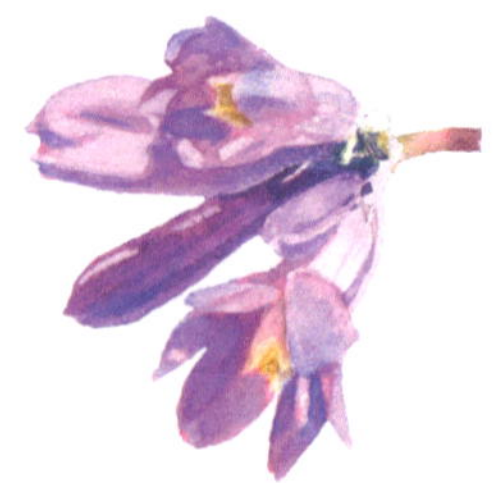

Blue Dicks
Dichelostemma capitatum

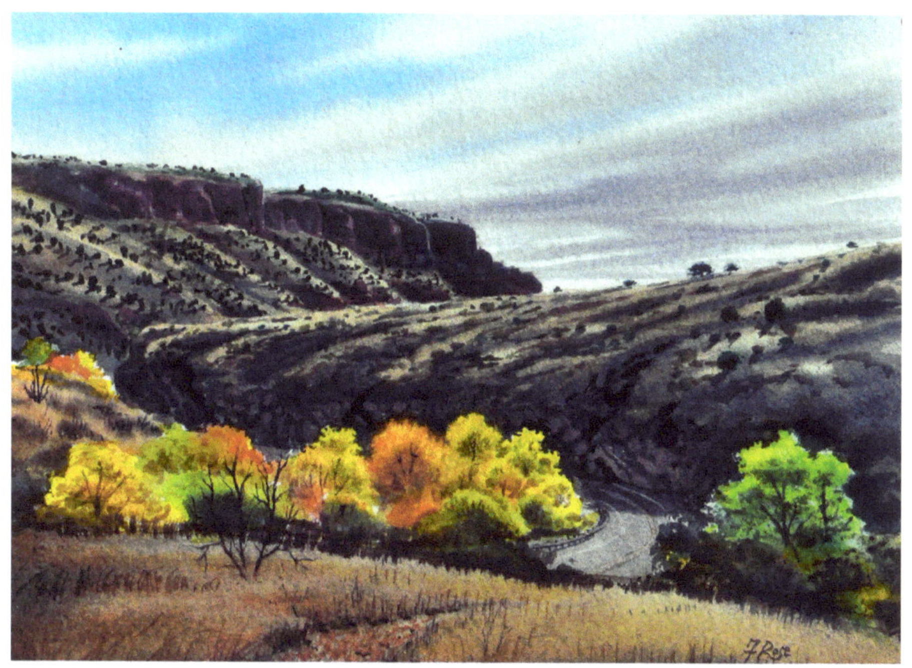

9. LEAVING MOLINO BASIN

The path in the middle bottom of this painting is part of the Arizona Trail in Molino Basin. Just behind the Ash and Cottonwood with their yellow fall leaves, is the toll booth that is no longer used. In just a few miles views of the Tucson valley will open up on your left.

My friend, Dave, and I hiked to the top of the ridge on the left, and found it packed with Shin Daggers, but offering spectacular views of the Tucson basin.

The steep and difficult route we followed seems to have been made for rock climbers.

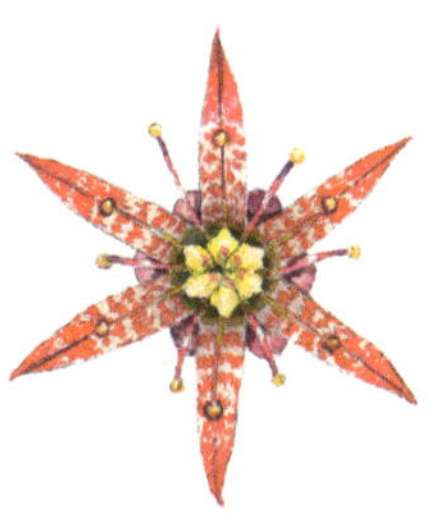

San Francisco River
Leather-Petal
Graptopetalum rusbyi

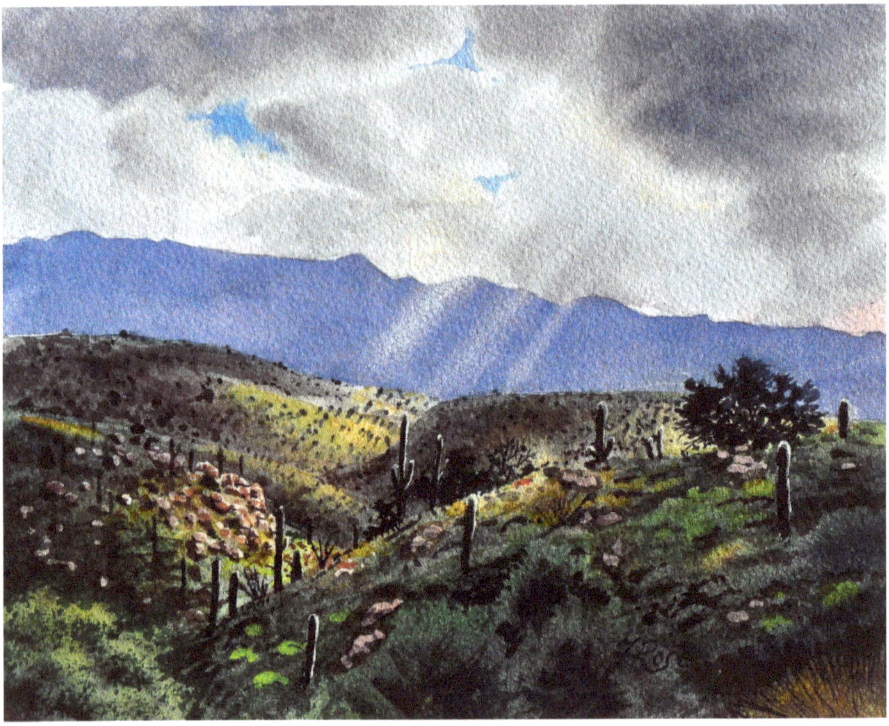

10. ALMOST HOME

Just after mile post four, we catch a view across Milagrosa canyon to Agua Caliente Hill and the Rincon mountains.

The sun is getting lower in the sky. We have returned to Saguaro country, and are almost home. It won't be long before we plan another trip up this incredible mountain range.

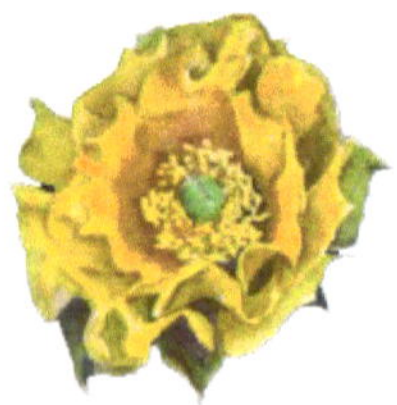

Engelmann Pricklypear
Opuntia engelmanii

Bibliography

1975 - *Trail Guide to the Santa Catalina Mountains* by Eber Glendening & Pete Cowgill - many editions

1987, 1994 - *Frog Mountain Blues* by Charles Bowden, U of A Press

1997, 2012 - *Plants of Arizona* by Anne Orth Epple

2003 - *Look to the Mountains* by Suzanne Hensel

2009 - *The Road to Mount Lemmon:* A Father, A Family, and the Making of Summerhaven by Mary Ellen Barnes and Tony Zimmerman

2013 - *A Natural History of the Santa Catalina Mountains*, Arizona by Richard C. Brusca and Wendy Moore
Arizona Sonoran Desert Museum Press

2016 - *A Guide to the Geology of the Santa Catalina Mounains, Arizona*
The Geology and Life Zones of a Madrean Sky Island by John V. Bezy
Arizona Geological Survey

2018 - *Annotated Flora of the Santa Catalina Mountains* by Jim Verrier

Other books by Frank S. Rose

2006 - Illustrations for *Herbal Medicine of the American Southwest* by Charles W. Kane

2011 - *Mountain Wildflowers of Southern Arizona* published by the Arizona Sonoran Desert Museum

2012 - *Mountain Trees of Southern Arizona* published by the Arizona Sonoran Desert Museum

2014 - *The Joy of Spiritual Living* by Frank S. Rose and Bob Maginel published by the Swedenborg Foundation

2015 - *The Joy of Spiritual Growth* by Frank S. Rose and Bob Maginel published by the Swedenborg Foundation

2016 - *The Art of Effective Preaching* co-authored with son, Dr. Jeremy Rose

2016 - Illustrations for *Bo and the Fly-away Kite* by Virginia Wade Ames

2018 - *Small Wonders* published by Hardy Perennial Press